MW01610756

Your TWIN SOUL Journey

A GUIDE TO EXPERIENCE ETERNAL, UNCONDITIONAL, HARMONIOUS, EMBODIED, AND SACRED LOVE AND UNION WITH YOUR DIVINE PARTNER

MONICA GRACE

Address inquiries to team@cardreadingqueen.com

Visit our website: CardReadingQueen.com

Library of Congress Cataloging-in-Publication Data

Grace, Monica.
Your twin soul journey

ISBN 978-1-63566-020-3 (pbk.)
ISBN 978-1-63566-019-7 (ebook)

Manufactured in the United States of America

First Edition
First Printing
Author: Monica Grace
Cover Design: Monica Grace

To my twin soul, I love you always.

TABLE OF CONTENTS

Welcome to the Twin Soul Journey   1

What is a Twin Soul?   20

Who is Your Twin Soul?   39

The Twin Soul Stages   61

The Twin Soul Trinity   79

Twin Souls and the Law of Attraction   98

Twin Souls and the Law of Polarity   126

How We Know the Twin Soul Trinity Exists   147

The Obstacles Blocking Your Twin
Soul Union   171

How To Heal and Love Yourself   188

The Reflection Journaling Practice   239

Setting Boundaries on the Twin Soul
Journey   248

Twin Soul Myths and Common Questions   279

Next Steps On Your Twin Soul Journey   328

About the Author

Acknowledgements

Chapter One

WELCOME TO THE TWIN SOUL JOURNEY

*E*x-Catholic, ex-agnostic, ex-scientist, ex-wife, recovering overachiever, corporate dropout... all of these descriptors have been influential in my research on how to find and keep the love of your life.

My name is Monica Grace and my first introduction to the concept of a twin soul—a.k.a. a twin flame, "the one," your "person," and your permanent partner in love—came from a Catholic priest back in 2006, though he didn't use those specific words. A few girlfriends reintroduced me to the concept a decade later in 2016, when I was trying to figure out how my supposed whirlwind romance turned marriage had turned into my greatest nightmare of a relationship.

I had believed that my ex-husband was "the one" when we got engaged only ten months after we started dating. Red flags popped up during our engagement and into marriage, but I persisted with the relationship because I had been told all about cold feet and I figured we would work it out—that's what married people did, right? I still loved him... but our relationship felt up and down and sometimes pretty toxic. We continued our crazy, tumultuous partnership for years after the wedding, through bouts of abuse on all levels along with lies, cheating, and addiction. I knew early on that the relationship was over, as it left me unfulfilled and acting out of character in so many ways. Having made a commitment, however, I felt too guilty to leave without doing absolutely everything possible to try to make it work.

As our relationship came to an obvious end, I wondered how we had even ever gotten into a relationship in the first place. We were so different! How could we have felt so connected and so sure, yet have ended up being wrong about it all?

From a young age, I had wanted a fairytale romance and to marry my true love... and at the same time, my approach to relationships was as naive as a 7-year old dressed as a Disney princess, twirling around in her living room, singing about walking with princes in dreams.

My relationship was not a fairytale, but it was a box of fireworks. We set the first few off and they lit up the sky like magic, electrifying us both into a quick engagement and marriage. And then we tried to hold onto the box, gripping the fireworks tightly in our hands until it eventually blew us (and the relationship) up.

After our divorce, I wanted to remarry and went searching for answers. I was trying to understand— how did I fall for this act so hard? And how do I make sure I never fall for it again? I felt like I had made a huge mistake by getting married and that the breakup was my fault. I wanted to unpack where I had gone so wrong. I also worried that I was a serial monogamist and addicted to being in a relationship. Did I even deserve love, after all my mistakes?

At the same time, I had completely lost faith in love, my future, my dreams of family, and any sense of a higher power. I didn't—and couldn't—trust myself until I understood my story and why it had gone so horribly different than what I intended.

I knew only one thing. I had wanted the fairytale so badly that I found someone who would repeat it back to me and reflect my dreams perfectly. He knew the pretty words to say and he easily painted swirly romantic dreams in my mind. I placed my trust in him quickly, but it never occurred to me that he might be lying for his own reasons. I bought the sales pitch based on being told what I wanted to hear, but I didn't check to see if my ex-husband was selling fantasy or the real thing.

After my ex-husband, I found a new relationship... but also found myself terrified that love just wasn't meant for me. If it was, I had no idea how to find the real and everlasting love I had been searching for my entire life.

And then, I discovered the truth about twin souls, and found a way to guarantee that I could find and hold onto a romantic, deeply fulfilling partnership for the rest of my life.

GETTING THE FAIRYTALE ROMANCE—FOR REAL

You may also be looking for a fairytale romance, a romance to end all romances, with a partner that you can be with permanently. You may have even met the right person, but hit a brick wall of communication issues, hot and cold behavior, and a relationship with lots of push and pull. Or maybe you are experiencing a deep but seemingly unrequited love and you're struggling to understand why your feelings are so intense for this particular person.

You are not alone in your questioning and you are not wrong to seek more information that could help you receive your dream of dreams and your perfect romantic relationship. It's more than possible, and this book will help you on your journey to getting everything that you desire.

You know this book is for you if you are experiencing any of the following symptoms:

- You are feeling immense pain over a previous relationship or breakup

- You are trying to understand this person from a 3D perspective and things are simply not adding up

- This person has left or moved on in some way, but your heart is saying that the two of you are not done

- All the things that worked in previous relationships receive the complete opposite results with this person

- This person is leaving you confused, overwhelmed, or crazy with nearly every major interaction you have with them

- Your friends are telling you or showing you that you need to move on, settle, or forget this person, but your gut is telling you not to

- You know this relationship is something different at the spiritual level

- You are familiar with the terms twin flame and twin soul, but your healing work is leaving you feeling uninspired and stuck

- You've experienced awakening and ascension before but this is on a completely different level that you're struggling to ground into

This book can help you through all of your relationship challenges with this person if:

- You have no idea what the twin soul journey

is, some idea what the twin soul journey is, or you've been on the twin soul journey for awhile

- You are really confused by some of the information and misinformation out there and have no idea how to discern what's real and what's not

- You didn't ask for the journey and didn't ask for this person to come into your life, but you find yourself here anyway

- You are looking for new insights and tools to move along in your journey

- You have been doing the healing work and you are tired of not seeing results

- You are losing faith in the concept of twin souls and wonder if you should just move on with your life

- You feel defeated by the twin soul journey and want to quit

I know the twin soul journey can seem painful, challenging, and sometimes unbearable. This book aims to help make your twin soul journey calm, productive, joyful, peaceful, and loving—just as it was always meant to be. In this book, I share with you my best tips and secrets for doing the healing work that actually works. I help you truly move through triggers, upsets, and blocks so you can cope with any challenges that come up and keep a level head during any twists and surprises on this journey.

This healing work is not just for twin souls and is not specific to twin souls. It's rooted in well-known and well-studied processes. I've taken all of my experience and knowledge of spirituality, ascension, and healing and applied many of the same tools and modalities to the twin soul relationship. As you learn this work, the tools I offer can also help you heal in all other areas of their life, including healing friendships and family tensions, making more money or advancing their career, finding their life purpose, designing a beautiful life, and manifesting more good things.

By the end of this book, I want for you:

- To feel less crazy, less alone, less frustrated, and less in pain over what you are experiencing right now

- To easily be able to shift into a higher perspective around what's really happening to you, for you, and with your twin soul

- To have a deeper understanding of the healing process and how to apply it to everything in your life

- To feel confident in resolving your relationship without any input from the other person, regardless of whether they are your twin soul or not

- To know that you deserve love, peace, beauty, and joy right now—and you can create it and attract your twin soul to you in the process

WHO CAN BE TRUSTED FOR TWIN SOUL TEACHINGS?

There is a lot out there about twin flames or twin souls, and to the uninitiated, it probably sounds like a *lot* of craziness.

To those who can get past unusual spiritual terms like ascension, divine, distorted, toxic, sacred, union, masculine and feminine, counterparts, and mirroring, there's still a minefield of information to navigate.

Who really understands this spiritual connection? Is it real? Is it a load of crock? And if I can really attain the love of my life, what are the actual rules and step-by-step?

The industry is currently in what I like to call the Wild West phase. Most of the people teaching twin soul work are at the beginning of a snowballing niche, a first wave if you will. Some teachers simply don't know much about the topic and are hopping on the bandwagon of a fun phrase they heard. Other teachers are jumping in with focus and making it up as they go, not thinking of the consequences of misinformation.

The result is the same: conflicting advice, illogical

rules, and frameworks that contradict themselves. Not to mention the toxic culture of spiritual teachers dissing other spiritual teachers as false prophets!

WHO AM I TO TEACH TWIN SOUL WORK?

In any industry, teachers can only instruct at the level as deep as they have gone to. I am no different and can only give you the pieces of this journey that I've already discovered myself. My story with spirituality and ascension starts with Catholicism, ventures through a period of agnosticism and atheism, gets exciting at the discovery of manifestation and the Law of Attraction, and makes a complete surprise left turn at the winding road of twin souls.

I've been studying tarot, astrology, manifestation, and other New Age concepts since 2012 and have been actively studying the concept of twin flames and twin souls and developing tools around it since 2017. I've successfully applied the twin flame concepts to my own divine union with my husband, Patrick, who I've been in a relationship with for ten years. Together in our union, we have tested the healing tools I share in this book, and I've coached others using the same concepts with great success.

I also work with my own coaches, healers, and channelers on a regular basis. I've shared my greatest teachers and how to find and work with them in the last chapter of this book.

A big part of my twin soul journey started with committing fully to my divine purpose—writing, teaching, entrepreneurship, and artistry. Much of that journey has prepared me for the twin soul journey, which only took me deeper into ascension. I remember the moment I made the fully embodied decision, felt through every cell in my body, to quit my 6-figure career as a marketing executive in the tech startup space to permanently pursue a career as a writer. I had worked so hard to fit into a box of what I thought people expected me to be, going to graduate school for business and pursuing high-end and well-paying opportunities, but I literally hit a point where I could no longer tolerate putting on the facade of happiness. My career was a dream career, but it was not *my* dream career. I was pretty sure that writers didn't make much money, but it didn't matter to me anymore. I was willing to be completely broke to be myself and do the work I knew I was meant to do on this earth.

I have been doing my divine purpose since 2011 and I haven't looked back. Taking this journey with my divine purpose first helped me depersonalize the twin soul journey early on. The twin soul journey is full of heightened emotion and challenging upsets, but I knew from the beginning that like the many writing rejections I had received when I was starting out in my new career, the upsets were not personal. This helped me to understand how twin souls actually worked and helped me get to the core concepts and frameworks quickly, which I'm now using to help others unite with their twin souls, too.

I don't believe in coincidences. Within weeks of committing fully to my divine purpose, I also started dating my twin soul. This makes sense as the ascension journey is all-encompassing and once you go all in with your higher power in one area, the rest are soon to follow. My husband and I had known each other before that for about a year, and while I felt an odd connection and friendship to him, I did not ever expect us to date, get married, and have a child together. My twin soul repelled me at first, and I even went so far as to tell him that we would never date, ever. This is surprisingly normal for twin souls when they meet, and we definitely had a lot of upsets as we came into our union. I share some of our stories in this book and more of them through the rest of my work.

Finally, I have spent the last two years sharing all of my knowledge about twin souls on my Card Reading Queen website, my Monica Grace Youtube channel, my Your Twin Soul Journey podcast, and my *Twin Soul Hearts in Union* book series. Teaching these concepts through my divine purpose has given me a new level of expertise as I'm working with a group of people who are dealing with challenges that are beyond the challenges I faced in my own journey. I currently create 100-episode seasons of twin soul content for Youtube, my podcast, and my blog every year. I also have books, workbooks, decks, and healing modality certifications to support you on the twin soul journey. You can always learn more about what I offer and how I can help you at my Card Reading Queen website.

While I work hard to be of as much assistance to you as possible on your twin soul journey, I strongly recommend that you take only what resonates with you from my work. It doesn't truly matter if I have the truth or not, as you will discover the truth of how the universe and twin souls work in your own time. Truth is truth. It is not something you nor I contain, it is something we both arrive at in our own perfect timing. We cannot control the truth, so I will greet you with a smile when we both arrive at the same destination.

In this book, I present what I understand to be the truth at this time. I am always going deeper in this journey, though, and will revise this book if I reveal myself to be wrong.

Do not get too caught up in any one way of doing healing work. You will inevitably have to walk your own path as no one can walk it for you. So take the path that makes the most sense to you, and take it at your own pace. As long as you are moving forward and doing your healing work, there is only one destination you can arrive at, and that's your union. The path to get there is fairly unimportant in comparison to all the growing you'll do in your twin soul union. Take the journey at the pace that feels good to you.

HOW DO TWIN SOUL TEACHINGS RELATE TO DATING COACHES, MARRIAGE COUNSELORS, AND OTHER LOVE-RELATED EXPERTS?

In my observation, twin soul work teaches the inner work that compliments what many other love-related experts share as the outer work.

If you look at the love, romance, and dating industry, you'll find several common problems paired with common solutions. Much of the dating industry focuses on how to interpret dating profiles and what they really mean when they do/don't do X, Y, and Z. The literature on long-term relationships is not much different, with tips on how to send the perfect text to get your ex back or the exact step-by-step solution which will keep your spouse from packing their bags.

Much of the advice given by love experts is rooted in psychology. For example, for the problem of getting your ex back — a popular search term — the expert always suggests a period of No Contact. During this period you are told to spend time with friends, explore your own interests, etc. All healthy things to do while getting over a breakup, of course.

This common advice is based on the idea that how you act will change how you feel over time. And yes, it's real and it works.

Tony Robbins speaks about this at his events. He asks his participants to act in a way a happy person would act, then act in a way a sad person would act, and compare. As he describes it on his website,

> "How do you change your state of mind, even when you're dealing with immense stress? The secret is in moving your body. Emotion is created by motion. In other words, emotions are linked to movement in our bodies. Observe your posture when you are happy, as opposed to when you are sad — or what you look like when you are angry, versus when you are elated.
>
> "There's a difference, right? Your body language sends signals to your brain, and the rest of the world, about how you're feeling and operating."

So the advice to get your ex-partner back is to effectively act like you are over the breakup, in hopes you start to feel like you are over the breakup.

Then, when you are in this calmer, healthier state of mind—when you've rid yourself of all the clinginess and bad behavior and toxicity and depression—you are encouraged to reach out to your ex for a coffee date, which may lead to renewed feelings.

OUTER WORK VS. INNER WORK

To me this is the outer work. And don't get me wrong, the outer work is fine and can get you some good results. I have nothing against content that teaches you the outer work as sometimes you just want to know exactly what to do and say to get a specific result.

But there's also something obvious that's missing: the inner work.

In the example with getting your ex back, there is inner work to actually getting over the original breakup. Sure, a person can feel they are over the breakup or over the person, but are they?

Or are there subconscious woundings and patterns that lie beneath the surface that will keep them obsessed with and clingy to their ex? Are there old behaviors that will lead to the same exact outcome if the two were to get back together? Are there false beliefs that will keep them facing the same challenges in their next relationship, should they move on?

For every problem that a human can have, there is always the outer work and the inner work. It's true for making a million dollars or for finding true love.

The outer work is good and instructive, but it doesn't create lasting transformation unless the inner work is completed too.

And at the same time, the inner work can make your body and spirit healthy again, but you still have to take the actions and live your life out loud in the physical.

The inner work is always healing. Call it shifting your mindset, setting new goals, healing your core wounds, changing your thought patterns, vibrating at a different frequency, eliminating false beliefs, casting magic spells, performing rituals, changing your energy, channeling something new... I could go on! Whatever you call it, when you do the inner work, the outer work comes naturally.

I believe that both the inner work and outer work are valuable. This book does get you real and outer world results, but it focuses on doing the inner work rather than the outer work. I want to help you make a lasting change and transformation around all your deepest fears and wounding, so that you not only find your perfect person who completely fulfills you, but also keep them around permanently.

Once you have made a true transformation from within, you can still use content that teaches the outer work to greater effect. But honestly, you probably won't need to because healed people attract everything they desire toward them easily and naturally, including their twin soul.

I have experienced running my life from a place of fear versus a place of love, from a belief in randomness versus a belief in magic, from an energy of getting things through hustle versus flow... and every time I come back to letting things unfold through the inner work. For me, the inner work is where life is most juicy. This book is ideal for you if you want

to go deeper into the ascension and twin soul journey, in order to create true and permanent change
within.

TAKE WHAT RESONATES FOR NOW

Just as I am only able to take you as deep into the
twin soul journey as I myself have gone, you are only
going to be able to receive this book at the level you
are ready for spiritually. Your higher power is never going to give you more information than you can
process, as that would not be compassionate to you
or helpful on your journey.

Most likely, if you are newer to the concept of
twin souls, you will need to read this book a few
times before all the chapters sink in completely. This
is because aligning to twin souls is a huge energy
shift for most people at the beginning of the journey, who are more likely currently aligned to the 3D
paradigm of relationships. There is no rush to do
this, and you will find plenty to receive on your first
read through. I have found that twin soul content
can feel completely fresh and inspiring again after a
long period—six months, a year—has passed. This is
because this truly is a spiritual journey and you truly
are retooling your vibration toward ascension just
by reading this book.

If you have been on this journey for a long time

already, you may be familiar with many of the topics and tools I discuss in the book, but I may present them in a new way that you've not heard before. This could help something click for you or push you forward on your twin soul journey. I always get my best insights and move through blocks in rapid succession by learning from someone else who is deeply grounded in the work. Are you ready to take the next step and have your next breakthrough?

JOURNALING PROMPTS

- Why did you pick up this book? What are you hoping to get out of it? Does it seem like a good fit so far?

- What do you think of the inner work versus the outer work?

- What are your concerns with twin soul teachings? Who do you trust in the twin soul community? How can you get strong results and break through on your twin soul journey?

FEELING STUCK?

- **Check out the free Your Twin Soul Journey podcast**, where I produce 100+ episode seasons every year on a variety of twin flame and twin soul topics. Listen on your commute to work, at your daily workout, or when you are doing chores around the house. You can learn more about the podcast here: http://cardreadingqueen.com/ytsj-podcast/

- **Subscribe to my free Card Reading Queen Youtube channel** where I post lots of tarot and astrology readings to help you understand the twin soul collective energies. You can find my channel here: http://cardreadingqueen.com/youtube

- **Find more books** about specific challenges you may be facing on the twin soul journey through my *Twin Soul Hearts in Union* book series. You can find the books we have on offer here: http://cardreadingqueen.com/books

Chapter Two

WHAT IS A TWIN SOUL?

A t 20 years old, I had just gotten out of a serious relationship with the love of my life at that time. I couldn't comprehend why we didn't work out, and I couldn't face the pain of losing the relationship. The only way I could walk away was to believe that this person didn't love me and I didn't love them, and that we didn't share the same dreams for our lives.

I deeply wanted my twin soul, even at this age, though I didn't have the specific words to describe it. Without fail, along came a young man who was willing to offer me my twin soul dreams—at least on the surface.

He believed we were soulmates and destined to be together. I was his dream girl, like the younger sister of his favorite television star, Kristin Kreuk. He had a mix of Josh Hartnett and Tom Welling going on. At the time, my favorite television show and the only one I watched was *Smallville*, a story that re-imagined Superman's life as the young teenager Clark Kent, played by Tom Welling, with a primary love interest played by Kristin Kreuk. I took it as a sign.

Everything seemed to fit with us and the romance came in a whirlwind. We started dating exclusively in January and by October of that same year we were engaged.

He said all the right things to me, playing exactly to all my fantasies, and it never occurred to me to stop and think—is the story he's telling me what I'm actually experiencing in my reality?

I imagine if you picked up this book, you have someone in mind that you think might be your twin soul. Perhaps you even feel sure of this person, or perhaps you are in a relationship with this person. Maybe you are fairly advanced on this journey and simply desire to go deeper with the person you are in a romantic relationship with, or maybe you are in separation with your twin soul and you are wondering how to reunite with them. Or perhaps you are still exploring the idea of twin souls and don't have anyone in mind. That's okay as well, as it's very easy to call in your twin soul whenever you feel ready.

No matter where you are on this journey and no matter what your situation, this chapter will help you go deeper into the concept of twin souls and help you identify your true twin soul.

WHAT IS A TWIN SOUL?

Your twin soul is the person you were created and meant to be with in life, according to your higher power—God, the Universe, Source, Spirit, your Creator, or life itself.

You likely desire your "person," or the one who you can partner with and spend your life with. By the Law of Attraction, because you desire it, your higher power has created it for you. The only reason you aren't experiencing this person in your physical reality is because you are instead believing in the illusion of separation from this person.

We go deeper into what a twin soul is throughout this book, so don't worry if the last several sentences haven't made much sense to you thus far.

At the physical level, your twin soul is you—but not a carbon copy of you physically. They are instead a carbon copy of you spiritually, similar to how identical twin siblings might be born together on earth.

You will look, think, and act differently from your twin soul, but at the spiritual level you are carbon copies. And just as identical twins on earth will continue to look the same as they grow up, due to having carbon copy physical DNA, you and your twin soul will also look the same at the spiritual level as you both grow up.

HOW DO TWIN SOULS WORK?

This concept is sometimes described as the twin

soul mirror, or the twin soul shared energy field, or even twin soul merging. There are lots of different attempts to describe the phenomenon that you may experience with your twin, but the one that has always been the most helpful to me is that you and your twin make the same core choices at the soul level at all times. (This is why I prefer the term "twin soul" to "twin flame," to constantly remind myself of how this works.)

When you make a choice at the soul level, your twin makes the same choice at the soul level. This does not mean that you make the same choice in the physical, or that your physical realities look the same.

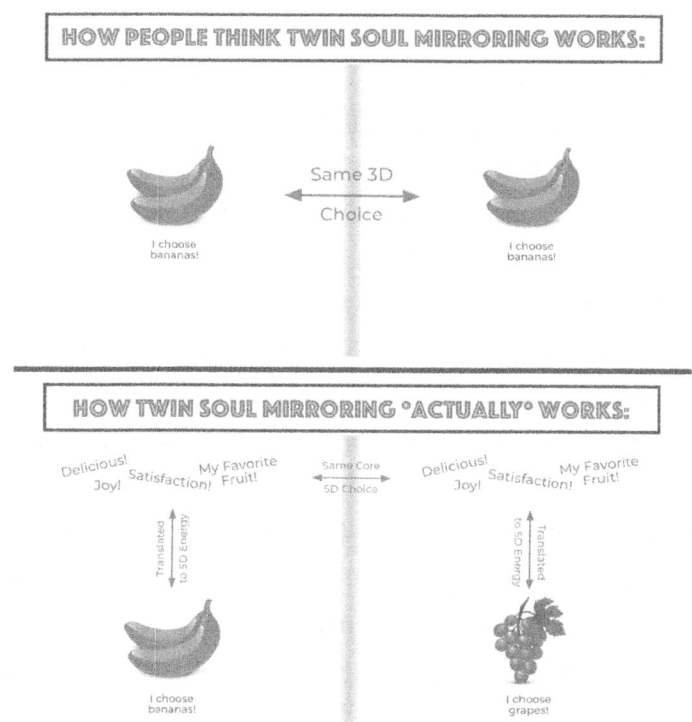

HOW PEOPLE THINK TWIN SOUL MIRRORING WORKS:

Same 3D Choice

I choose bananas!

I choose bananas!

HOW TWIN SOUL MIRRORING "ACTUALLY" WORKS:

Delicious! Satisfaction! My Favorite Joy! Fruit!

Same Core 5D Choice

Delicious! Satisfaction! My Favorite Joy! Fruit!

Translated to 5D Energy

Translated to 5D Energy

I choose bananas!

I choose grapes!

Most people think that your twin soul makes the same choice as you in the 3D. For example, some people on this journey believe that if they end their 3rd party relationship, then their twin soul will also break things off with their partner.

What really happens is that whatever decision they make on the 3D level is just a symbol of their inner world. So we have to go deeper: why did they end their third party relationship? Perhaps it was because they were feeling clingy or controlling toward their twin soul. This energy gets translated to the 5D, and then their counterpart mirrors their 5D choice.

Now, their counterpart is also making a life-changing clingy and controlling decision. This could be anything—a big move, a career change, getting engaged, or even calling in a child!

This is not to say don't end your 3rd party situation, but rather to say that you can't control your twin soul journey by doing the outer work. Your twin soul is not mirroring your 3D decisions, but rather mirroring your inner world and energy. The physical can look much different for twin souls, but they are healing the exact same core blocks and wounding at the spiritual level every time. This is why this journey is truly about doing the inner work. You can't get your twin soul union by controlling your outer reality... just ask the people who have tried and instead pushed their twin soul even further away in the physical as a result.

WHAT IS A TWIN SOUL?

WHAT IS THE TWIN SOUL UNION?

Your twin soul meets you at every level: mental, physical, spiritual, emotional, mentor/mentee, best friend, family member, and romantic lover. You are meant to be with them at all eight of these levels, though some of these levels may develop before others.

The reason they meet you at every level is because they are designed to be with you permanently. This means that they can completely fulfill you and all your desires in the area of romantic partnership. Many choose to seek their twin soul union first because much of the rest of life is built on who you spend your life with or marry.

You can assess your relationship with your twin soul using my 8x8 Shape of Your Union tool. To use this bullseye, draw eight circles and make eight divisions. You can label each division with one of these categories, then rate that area of your relationship from 1-8. If you see areas that are low in this relationship, look at how you can increase your satisfaction in those areas, not through your twin soul, but through yourself or your higher power.

I find this tool extremely useful to notice the places where I am not romancing myself, not being a friend to myself, not mentoring myself, not engaging myself emotionally, and so on. This is my first clue that my union isn't where I desire it to be, and my first point of investigation to see why that is. I use this tool to do a weekly or monthly check in on my union in order to hold it in my reality.

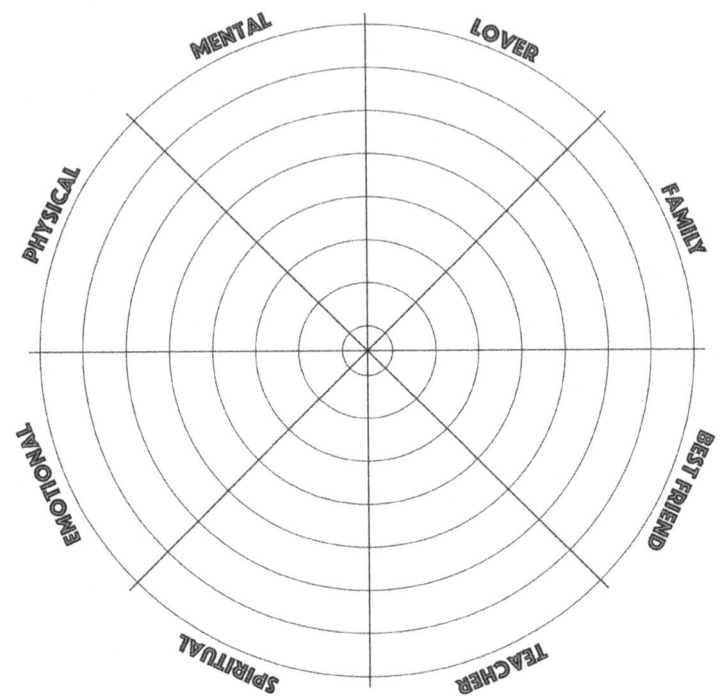

ARE TWIN SOULS RARE?

Have you heard that there are only 144,000 twin souls on the planet? And that they are all Aquarian star seeds from the planet Nimba!

All jokes aside, twin souls are not rare, and anyone who desires a twin soul is by definition the twin soul to the person they desire. This is due to the Law of Attraction. If you have a desire in your heart,

WHAT IS A TWIN SOUL?

it is out there for you and already yours, you only have to heal the separation between you and it. So if you desire a twin soul, your twin soul is out there—and because the two of you are meant to be together, they also desire and love you.

Also due to the Law of Attraction, your twin soul is here on earth, incarnated in the same lifetime as you. There are only a few exceptions:

- You are younger and your twin is not born yet

- You are older and your twin has passed on

- You truly at your core do not desire to receive an expression of love through a romantic relationship

If you desire something in your heart, it is here on the planet and available to you at any time. Your higher power doesn't create impossible desires within you, as to do so would serve no purpose and waste your energy. Why would your higher power want to waste your energy? Trust that if you desire it, it's because you are meant for it and it is meant for you—especially when it comes to your twin soul.

The belief that twin souls are rare is really only a wounding and desire to be special, chosen, and different. This is something you can heal, because you are special, chosen, and different at a spiritual level—but only to your twin soul. You each have a unique relationship to your higher power as well, which only means that you relate uniquely to God, the Universe, Source, Spirit, your Creator, or whatever other term you prefer.

What is rare, though? Twin souls in embodied love and union is rare or at least, unusual, because most people settle down with soulmates. Society tells us to find someone with the traits of a soulmate because twin souls is not a widely accepted concept yet. Eventually, enough people will understand and believe in twin souls/flames and society will shift to an energy where everyone is trying to unite with their twin soul instead of coming together with a soulmate.

ARE TWIN SOULS REAL?

I believe wholeheartedly in twin souls because I have seen a twin soul couple in its purest form on the other side, beyond the veil. When I met this couple, they were peaceful, loving, and calm. Their energies were distinct from one another while at the same time entwined in each other. It was difficult to see where one of them ended and the other began. They spoke to me with one consciousness, but all the while I could tell they were two beings; they were simply that synchronized. They answered all my questions, and right before they left me, they coated me in this liquid gold love.

I could have bottled that love and sold it and become a multi-millionaire, easily. It reached every cell in my body, loving me in places that no human, including myself, had loved me before. This is what twin soul love in its purest form feels like.

Every other love I'd felt up to this point paled in comparison. Even the unconditional love of my parents felt terribly human in comparison. There was an emptiness in that love that this golden love had filled. And though I tried my hardest to go back to the golden love in the days that followed, physical reality eventually took over. With each attempt to access that love, it dulled and faded and became harder to hold until I could no longer fully feel it in my body.

After this experience, I went all in on the twin soul journey for myself. I had been curious about it for awhile after coming across it so many times and trying to learn about it, but this was the moment for me. I wanted to feel that love again. I wanted to experience a closeness so deep that I could literally see my consciousness in another person, because we were the same. I wanted my twin soul.

It's important to know that this is my story and the proof that I needed to believe that twin souls exist. I have since seen twin souls in the physical and the energy is similar, though heavier and mired in separation most of the time. I've seen twin soul pairs that are completely in love but struggle to come together or commit to each other, as well as twin soul pairs that deeply repel each other, despite their similarities. I have also applied the concepts to my own relationship and gone deeper with my twin soul as a result.

You are not meant to believe in twin souls just because I have seen them or have told you they exist. No one can tell you that twin souls are real because no one can convince you of the truth. You can only discern for yourself whether twin souls are real through your own exploration of the subject and what rings true for you.

You are likely drawn to the concept of twin souls, but only you can take the journey you are meant to take with it. It's safe to explore twin souls without having all the answers. The answers are revealed to you as you commit more deeply to the journey, which is unique to you and your twin soul.

If you are still struggling with whether to commit to your twin soul journey, remember that nothing can be lost through the commitment. If it doesn't work out the way you want, you will still heal and find more peace through completing the inner work.

WHERE DID TWIN SOULS COME FROM?

The origin story of twin souls, including how twin souls came to be in separation, can be found in none other than the story of Adam and Eve. Before I proceed further... most people have tremendous blocks against the story of Adam and Eve due to religious and societal conditioning. In truth though, this metaphor is a powerful way to understand how twin souls work, if you are willing to release all of your wounding around what you think the story is.

The gist of the story is that God created Adam and Eve, twin soul counterparts with masculine and feminine energies, respectively, and placed them in heaven—the Garden of Eden. Eve was tempted to eat from the Forbidden Tree of Knowledge and this spiraled into both Adam and Eve choosing separation consciousness. The story specifically shows how Adam and Eve choose separation consciousness through the six core wounds: abandonment, betrayal, control, injustice, shame, and rejection.

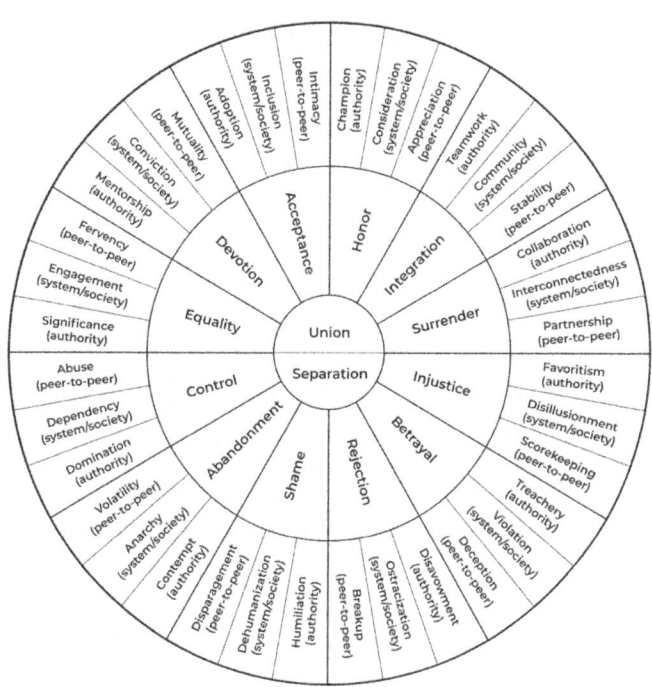

These six core wounds are just different shades of separation consciousness, which is just the lack of union consciousness. You can shift out of these core wounds by shifting to the core healing: integration, devotion, surrender, equality, honor, and acceptance. The ascension process, which the twin soul journey is simply one access point to, is how humanity is healing separation consciousness back to unity consciousness.

Whether Adam and Eve truly existed is irrelevant; the metaphor is a critical piece to understanding what the twin soul journey is and how twin souls came to exist.

You will sometimes see Plato referred to in explaining what twin souls are or where the concept comes from. The Greeks ultimately believed that humans had been split into two, and each half was trying to reunite with its other half.

Plato writes in his *Symposium*,

> "Love is born into every human being; it calls back the halves of our original nature together; it tries to make one out of two and heal the wound of human nature. Each of us, then, is a 'matching half' of a human whole...and each of us is always seeking the half that matches him."

While Plato is correct that we are calling pieces of ourselves back to us through healing wounds, so we can be restored to our original divine human nature, he mistakenly places those pieces outside of ourselves and into another person. In truth, your twin soul is not someone outside of you that you need to get back to in order to complete yourself. You are whole already—that is the illusion that the twin soul journey attempts to shatter.

Your union is actually inside of you, in your relationship with your higher power—God, the Universe, Source, Spirit, your Creator, or whatever name you prefer. When this relationship is in union specifically in the area of a love partnership and romance, your twin soul appears as the physical manifestation of your relationship with your higher power.

This is no different from how the money you desire manifests once you heal your separation, blocks, and limiting beliefs from it. The concept doesn't change even when your desire is another human being, and there are no issues around free will that can get in the way (for more on free will on the twin soul journey, see my comments in Chapter 6).

This is the Law of Attraction, and it is a foundational piece of the twin soul journey. The Law of Attraction states that anything that you have the desire for already exists and is yours; all you have to do is heal your separation from it.

The Law of Attraction cannot be traced back nearly as far as Plato or the story of Adam and Eve. It is a fairly new school of thought that has been around for 100-150 years. The Law of Attraction is part of an evolution and ascension of the world, from its former understanding rooted in duality, to its coming understanding rooted in union. I go into more detail about the Law of Attraction in Chapter 6.

WHAT IS THE TWIN SOUL JOURNEY?

The twin soul journey is an ascension path to choosing love and leaving the illusion of your reality behind. Many believe and will tell you that the journey is painful and hard, but in truth it's deeply peaceful and simple. This particular illusion comes from the way the twin soul journey triggers all your pain and wounding that's buried in your subconscious. It must come to the conscious to be released, so that you can feel a permanent sense of peace, love, and joy in that same place. This restores you to your natural state.

Why do we need to bring pain and wounding to the conscious? As you push pain to the subconscious, it gives you an illusion of control, but it's just that: an illusion. The illusion is what will drive your emotions, thoughts, and actions, right into a life that feels completely foreign to you.

"When it rains, it pours." Have you ever experienced your life falling apart around you all at once?

I have, when I got divorced from my ex-husband. As scary and challenging as it was to watch everything I had built crumble around me, there was also a freedom to it. I was releasing all that was not and had never been meant for me permanently. I no longer needed to hold on to the false and temporary highs that had kept me numbed out to what I truly wanted in life.

It seemed like as my life with him fell apart, I fell back into myself again in so many other areas— my career, my home, my dreams. Permanence feels good—in fact, it's the only thing that feels good.

When I thought about the differences between building a temporary life based on ephemeral highs and the permanent life I have now, I saw that my life with my ex-husband also came together very easily. This was because we came together out of wounding, and we spiraled into situations, homes, and jobs out of that same wounding. But when I found myself in a one-bedroom highrise with no furniture, no food, and at the bottom of a wine bottle four nights out of seven, I knew my life had really taken a wrong turn. That wounding had led me astray, big time.

Having wounding stuck in your subconscious is like having magical gremlins in your GPS or navigation system, trying to lead you astray. Staying in this state will only purport the illusion of separation from the life you desire and the life you are designed for, which includes your twin soul.

As we release this pain and wounding, we are

restored to our natural state as divine, unique, and whole beings. We are each designed with specific preferences, desires, skill sets, and goals. Releasing the pain and wounding (a.k.a. the separation from our desires) gets us into alignment with our true design—the design of our higher power. Once we understand our true design, we can move into the life that was designed for us by our higher power, which includes romance with our true twin soul.

AM I ON THE TWIN SOUL JOURNEY?

You have likely picked up this book through divine timing and order, as information comes to you right as you need it. Most likely, you are on the twin soul journey solely due to this fact. If you have any question or concern that you might not be, consider this: do you desire the love of your life, "the one," your "person," and the soul that you are meant to spend the rest of your life (and any lives thereafter) with? If so, you are on the twin soul journey. If, however, you have no true desire for that level of love, then you may not be and you can close the book.

Does the thought of having the love of your life cause you any level of anxiety or fear? In that case, you are probably still on the twin soul journey, but your fears are holding you back from pursuing this journey wholeheartedly.

It truly doesn't matter and you don't need to know for sure that you are on the journey to explore it. I'm an avid hiker and I usually don't know what hiking trail I'm on, especially once I get out into the woods. But I still take the next step and enjoy the scenery all the same. You can enjoy this book and take any additional steps you are called to without feeling wholeheartedly committed to uniting with your twin soul at this time.

JOURNALING PROMPTS

- What does your union truly look like? Use the 8x8 Shape of Your Union tool if it resonates with you.

- What areas of your relationship do you desire to work on? How can you give yourself the love and peace you desire in each area?

- Are you willing to take the next step on your twin soul journey, even without having all the answers?

FEELING STUCK?

- **Grab the 8x8 Shape of Your Union printable.** This is an amazing way to take stock of your union. You can use this printable monthly or weekly to get in tune with what aspects of your union are doing well or lacking. Grab the printable at http://cardreadingqueen.com/8x8

- **Watch the Adam and Eve video/podcast/ blog post** where I break down the metaphor of Adam and Eve and show exactly how they chose separation consciousness through the six core wounds. Check it out at http://cardreadingqueen.com/adam-eve-core-wound-breakdown

- **Check out the Core Wound Wheel Cheat Sheet** which helps you identify and name the wounding you are experiencing now. http://cardreadingqueen.com/core-wound-wheel/

Chapter Three

WHO IS YOUR TWIN SOUL?

The young man I met at 20 years old did not end up being my twin soul. He had given me the story I wanted in words, but I found myself ignoring the red flags during our engagement and trying to wrangle myself into a smaller and smaller box during our marriage.

Being with my ex-husband felt like being slowly suffocated by a Python snake. By the end of our marriage, all of my ebullience and creativity had been squeezed out of me, leaving me a lifeless, empty skin. In the relationship, I had experienced abuse, manipulation, lies, cheating, and addiction. In the aftermath of the relationship, I found that the cage was open, but I wasn't truly free.

It took many years and the help of my husband, Patrick, to heal through all the pain and trauma I experienced during this relationship. It took many more years to understand that at the spiritual level, my ex-husband was a karmic twin, meant to help me clear some serious toxicity from my own energy field. In this chapter, I explain more about the various labels that are put on relationships on the twin soul journey and how you can narrow in on who your twin soul is—and who they are not.

WHO IS MY TWIN SOUL?

Are you hoping to see a name printed in big, bold letters here on this page or in this e-ink? (And wouldn't that be nice? Seriously!)

As you probably suspected, I'm not able to confirm your twin soul for you. However, I can point you in the right direction, and that is truly all you need at the moment.

You may already know your twin soul—perhaps you met them previously or even dated them in the past. You may be searching for your twin soul, or you may be convinced down to your bones of your twin soul's identity. The person who you think is your twin soul may change over time, as false twins, karmics, and catalysts are revealed (more on this later in the chapter).

In truth, your twin soul is going to be revealed to you over time and through your own healing work. Remember, this journey is about uncovering your own pain and wounding to reveal yourself to you.

As long as you are doing your healing work, your twin soul is coming toward you. As you grow closer to yourself, your twin soul will arrive in your reality. They must, by the Law of Attraction. Remember, they already exist in the world simply because you desire them. You only need to heal the separation between you and your desire: your twin soul union.

WHY DO I NEED MY TWIN SOUL?

So why do you need your twin soul at all? You don't *need* your twin soul to be happy—that's one of the core lessons that this journey teaches you—but you do *desire* your twin soul. That is why this journey matters, because your *desires* matter. You are meant to be one with all of your desires, and as you heal your ability to truly love yourself, you will come to see that you are more than worthy of everything you want. This twin soul journey and work brings you the peace, love, and joy inside you which you are meant to experience and share with your twin soul.

As you are doing the spiritual work, you can use anyone and anything as a mirror, but it will be extremely helpful to you to mirror your upsets from your twin soul or the person you think is your twin soul specifically. The reason is that these upsets are core to your journey and amplified through your twin soul. You can heal any upset through anyone and anything, but your twin soul will trigger your core upsets around having the romantic relationship of your dreams. The most direct path to your healing is through your twin soul or the person you think is your twin soul.

That's why it truly doesn't matter who your twin soul is. It's safe to assume the person you think is your twin soul is your twin soul and follow the spiritual thread of your relationship until they are revealed otherwise.

What does this mean, specifically? It means that whatever they are doing that is upsetting you, you can use them as a mirror and heal through it to restore the relationship, which is really just a relationship with yourself, to peace.

Additionally—and this is a bit tricky—if you have two potential people in mind and you truly don't know which is your twin soul, you can follow both relationship threads from a spiritual perspective until one or neither is revealed as your twin soul. This is how you surrender to whatever your higher power reveals to you to be the truth.

BUT HOW DO I KNOW WHO MY TWIN SOUL IS?

I asked myself this question frequently during my first year or so on the journey. At the time, I was still struggling to understand and believe in twin souls to begin with, so I was *not* down to hear about how if I just do my healing work, my twin soul would appear.

It's totally fine if you are in this same space and just want to know who your twin soul is. This confirmation can be validating, encouraging, and supportive in sticking to your journey. An analogy that comes to mind is weight loss—sure, you may know that you're improving your health through better lifestyle choices, but you still want to see the numbers on the scale go down.

The three most popular ways to verify your twin soul's identity are:

STRESS TESTING

Sometimes called muscle testing and sometimes performed with an exterior object, like a pendulum, stress testing is a simple way to ask yes/no questions or confirm true/false statements and get clear answers. The idea is to circumvent your logical mind and allow your physical body to have a visible and verifiable gut reaction to a question or statement.

INSTRUCTIONS:

1. Stand with your legs shoulder-width apart. Allow your body to rock front to back, back to front. Let your body be loose.

2. Set the parameters of your test: for example, swaying or stepping forward is "true" while

swaying or stepping backward is "false."

3. Choose a statement you know the answer to so you can test to make sure your "human pendulum" works. For example, you can say out loud or in your mind, "My name is _____."

4. Stand tall, then let your body relax and rock.

5. If you fall forward, the statement is true. If you fall backward, the statement is false.

You may want to perform this test multiple times and play around with different statements or questions. This test helps you connect to your intuition, which is an important compass on the twin soul journey.

THE 3X3X3 SIGNS AND SYNCHRONICITIES TEST

Sometimes called a 72-hour test, and with many variations, this test uses specific signs and synchronicities of your choosing to verify your twin soul or anything else you want to verify. This test is meant to show you that you have constant and foolproof communication with the Universe—also known as God, Source, Spirit, your Creator, or your higher power. In fact, if you are struggling to communicate with your twin soul, which is common on this journey, you only need to heal your understanding of how you communicate with the Universe. The Universe always responds to your communication, which is a concept I go deeper into in both Chapter 6: Twin Souls and the Law of Attraction.

INSTRUCTIONS:

1. Choose a yes/no question. For example, "Is _____ my twin soul?"

2. Set your 3x3x3 parameters. Ask for three signs of your choosing, three times each, over three days to confirm your query. Write this out in an email to yourself so you don't forget the details. Send it to yourself so you have an exact timestamp of when you made your request to the Universe.

3. Over the next 72 hours, whenever you see a sign that is in your three signs, take a photo or screenshot on your computer, phone, or other device. Save it to a specific folder on your device, preferably using a synced space like Dropbox or Google Photos so everything is collected in one place.

4. At the end of 72 hours, check to see if you received all nine signs to give you a "yes!" to your query.

Every time I have used this test I always receive my signs, because the Universe is an extremely efficient communicator and always receives and reflects your message.

YOUR TWIN SOUL UNION CORE VALUES LIST

Sometimes called a Love List, Soulmate Wish List, or Partnership Manifestation List, your Twin Soul Union Core Values List is a powerful spiritual tool that was first popularized in the dating community. The way I teach this tool is to create a list of your core values that you want to experience not just in your relationship, but also in your life. This includes the type of relationship you want, the way you want your life purpose to unfold, how you want to live and build your home, and how you want to express yourself in the physical world.

INSTRUCTIONS:

1. Make a list of everything you want in your life, specifically around your twin soul union.

2. You can design your list however you want and include anything and everything that is important to you on it.

3. Don't make your list based on any specific person; instead, base it on only yourself and what you desire.

4. When you are done with your list, you will

have not only a list of everything you want in another person and your dream life with that person, but also a list of everything you yourself desire to be.

5. As you step deeper into becoming the person you describe in your list, your true twin soul has no choice but to arrive in your reality as your list describes.

I have made my list several times and consider it to be an ongoing, workable document. I've shared my 2018 list and 2020 list in a printable bundle that I offer through my website. In those more detailed instructions I share everything I've learned about using the Twin Soul Union Core Values List, including why the list needs regular updating and how to go very deep into the list with 10 critical questions you must consider.

GOING DEEPER TO VERIFY YOUR TRUE TWIN SOUL'S IDENTITY

These are three of the most popular ways you will find to verify your twin soul's identity. If you would like to go much deeper into the topic and learn the nine ways I've discovered through my work, I have a book called *Find Your Twin Soul: The Nine Foolproof*

Ways You Can Recognize and Confirm Your Twin Soul (Twin Soul Hearts in Union #2). In this book, I go into great detail on the nine ways you can recognize and verify your twin soul's identity, with crystal clear instructions on how to perform each test and the advantages and disadvantages of each one.

TWIN SOULS VS. SOULMATES VS. KARMIC TWINS

You may be wondering, what makes a twin soul different from a soulmate? Or perhaps you've heard of the term "karmic twin" and are wondering what that's all about?

Your twin soul is one of the permanent relationships that you are meant to have here on earth. There are also several neutral relationships that you may encounter, along with many relationships that you experience in order to heal and release.

PERMANENT RELATIONSHIPS

There are some people you are meant to go through life with. These people fall into two categories: your twin soul and your soul family.

YOUR TWIN SOUL

Your twin soul or twin flame is your ideal partner. They match you and meet you on a mental, physical, emotional, spiritual levels. They are your greatest student and your greatest teacher, your best friend and your perfect romantic lover, and your chosen family member. You are meant to live your life with your twin soul, as they are the only person perfectly tuned to your design and how you grow over your lifetime.

You are not able to grow apart from your twin soul because the two of you are cut from the same soul cloth and have carbon copy soul DNA. You make the same core choices and heal the same wounding throughout your lives. As you grow toward your higher power, they grow toward your higher power, and you also grow toward your twin soul.

YOUR SOUL FAMILY

Your soul family is a group of people that you are also meant to ascend with. They are similar to your twin soul but are not meant to be your perfect romantic partner—they are more like close siblings. You have similar soul DNA to your soul family, but they are not your twin soul.

Your soul family can nearly meet you on many of the same levels that your twin soul can meet you. This can sometimes be confusing to you as a human, and you can find yourself in a deep connection or even romantic relationship with someone in your soul family as a result. In spiritual truth, your relationship to your soul family is meant to be that of family, not romance. Your soul family is around to love and support you, even though you don't make the same core choices. They are compatible with you in interests and purpose.

No matter how great your parents and siblings were, your earthly family has likely left you mired in drama and wounding. Like your twin soul, your soul family can only interact with you from a place of love. You may experience soul family members who you repel or who repel you as a result. Additionally, your soul family desires for you to reunite with your twin soul in the physical, as when twin souls unite, it makes it significantly easier for everyone in their soul family to reunite with their twin souls too.

When you meet another in your soul family, you have actually gained two siblings, as their twin soul is also a part of your soul family. Because your soul family is so similar to you, it's even possible that members of your soul family have entered the twin soul journey at or around the same time as you.

If you were to roll out a sheet of cookie dough and use each of your cookie cutters twice, this would be what your soul family looks like. You would have very similar and compatible cookies, with each cookie having a carbon copy partner. Your soul family members are the cookies, and your twin is cut from the same cookie cutter as you.

NEUTRAL RELATIONSHIPS

Your neutral relationships are people you have experienced for a season or possibly a lifetime. These people fall into two categories: soulmates and kindred souls.

SOULMATES

A soulmate is someone who is there for you at certain seasons of your life. They will match you on some levels, which creates the initial attraction. More likely though, as you dig deeper into your relationship with a soulmate, the bonds between you are actually around your wounding, not around love.

Being in a romantic relationship with a soulmate feels like you essentially have to walk on eggshells or only express a small part of yourself to make the relationship work. The crux of the soulmate relationship is compromise, in that you usually must compromise some part of yourself to maintain the relationship. There is also a give and take to the relationship that makes it work, but if one party were to stop this exchange, the relationship would fall apart easily. Ultimately, you are bonded to a soulmate through wounding and exchange, which can sometimes pass for love, but eventually feels bad and stale.

You may grow with a soulmate for a time, but you will both eventually go your own ways. Your twin soul makes the same core choices as you, and your soul family makes complimentary core choices. A soulmate does not make the same core choices as you though, and in truth they are spiritual strangers and easily interchangeable.

It is safe to release a soulmate and natural to do so as you heal communication, codependency, and neediness. You may heal with a soulmate but usually need to give up a soulmate to pursue your journey further. A soulmate will always fall away effortlessly once you truly stop compromising yourself to maintain the relationship, because the soulmate is no longer receiving what they wanted from you.

Even if you released a soulmate "prematurely," you would always receive another soulmate to teach you the lesson because there is no true permanent spiritual connection between a soulmate and you. A soulmate is a tool used by your higher power to help you heal, and nothing more.

KINDRED SOULS

The kindred soul is essentially a spiritual acquaintance. This can be true even if you get to know the person well through a situation, like a friend group, a school or program you both attend, work projects, or even a familial connection.

With the kindred soul, you usually don't have a true connection built on spiritual truth or foundation, which is why these friendships and relationships fall apart so easily. An example might be a coworker who you chat with every day about work projects. If you no longer work at the same company, there is no longer a connection between the two of you!

A kindred soul can also be brought into your life

to help trigger or reveal something to you; however, this is rarely something that you couldn't reveal through your main relationships already. For example, your boss could reveal a wounding you are working through, but that wounding pattern is likely also present with your parents or other caregivers in your life.

It is safe to release a kindred soul and safe to never invest your energy into a kindred soul to begin with, once you are able to correctly identify them. This doesn't mean that you are unkind, rude, or cold to a kindred soul, but rather that you interact with them from a place of non-attachment.

DISTORTED RELATIONSHIPS

Your distorted relationships are people who are helping you get into your union faster by pointing you in the direction of your healing. In the moment, these connections usually feel either really good or really bad—there's not much in between.

Either way, a distorted relationship is something to approach with gratitude, not frustration. Distorted relationships help you refine what you want in your twin soul and help you find unconditional love for yourself. While there is no foundation to these distorted relationships (thus they cannot last—a good thing!), they help you build the foundation within yourself. All of the healing you do stays with you.

These people fall into three categories: catalysts, false twins, and karmic twins.

CATALYSTS

A catalyst is someone you have strong romantic feelings for that turns out to not be your twin soul. Most likely, they are the person who caused you to seek out twin soul or twin flame work. You usually learn quickly that they are not your twin soul and you easily release them from your reality.

FALSE TWINS

A false twin is someone you believe to be your twin soul for the majority of your healing journey. Unlike with the catalyst, who is revealed quickly to not be your twin soul (they vibrate out of your reality when their purpose of introducing you to twin soul work is over), the false twin is revealed to you slowly and you usually heal a number of major blocks with them. The purpose of a false twin is:

- To help you move through your blocks and upsets fast so you can be with your twin soul sooner

- To protect your union from accumulating additional wounding and distrust that will complicate the connection or slow down union

You can identify a false twin when you heal all the things they are showing you, but their behavior doesn't change. They are not making the same core choice as you. Over time, you realize that there is nothing deep there and never will be because they simply aren't you; you were attracted to them largely through your wounding. You usually feel no lasting hard feelings as you release a false twin, as they are not a bad person and they didn't do anything wrong, they just don't match your vibration and core values as you continue to heal.

KARMIC TWINS

A karmic twin is a truly toxic false twin that shows you the darkest parts of yourself. This person will consistently choose fear over love at every turn, regardless of what you do or heal. Patterns of abuse, manipulation, lies, and other distorted energies may plague your relationship with this person.

A karmic twin only knows how to take. They are often lying to you about themselves to get you into a false twin relationship. This can make it tricky to figure out who they really are, as well as who you really are! While the other two distorted relationships are largely about you being mistaken about who you are, this one is specifically about seeing where you are abusing yourself.

Some people believe that a karmic twin comes into your life due to past karma. While I have found that looking into your past lives through readings can be helpful to rid yourself of the karmic twin energetically, this distorted relationship is ultimately no different than any other. You have attracted it because you have a distorted love for yourself and you desire to heal those patterns within quickly.

GOING DEEPER INTO YOUR SPIRITUAL RELATIONSHIPS

A label is not necessary to understand your relationships, but I have personally found it helpful to categorize my relationships in order to move forward. I have found that having these labels can help you navigate your twin soul journey much more easily because you can get so much closer to understanding who your twin soul is when you understand who they are not.

I go much deeper into each of these labels in my book, *Twin Souls vs. Soulmates vs. Karmic Twins: How To Identify, Understand, and Interpret Every Spiritual Connection in Your Life To Find Harmony in Your Twin Soul Union (Twin Soul Hearts in Union #3).* In the book, I spend an entire chapter on each relationship and offer 10-15 detailed signs to tell whether the person you're thinking of is a twin soul, soulmate, karmic twin, and so on.

I know what it's like to feel anxiety, frustration, and lack of peace over not knowing who is who on this journey, which is why I've dedicated an entire book to the topic.

CAN I HAVE MULTIPLE TWIN SOULS?

It's possible to have multiple twin souls, but it's rare and is usually only discovered after coming into union with your first twin. Then, the two of you together discover that there is an additional twin (or more).

If you are coming at this question from a place of, "I'm in love with two or more people and can't choose," there could be few things at play:

- **One of them is a twin soul and the other(s) is a soulmate, false twin, or karmic twin -** In this case, I find that the one who is moving toward you as you heal is the likely next step in your twin soul journey. I recommend choosing one of these souls (the one you have the strongest relationship with) and focusing on this journey as if that person were definitely your one and only twin soul. Through this, you will heal a ton that benefits your twin soul journey. If you are wrong, you will clear your karma with this person and eventually vibrate away from each other.

- **You are on the twin soul journey but none are twin souls -** It's possible that you haven't met your twin soul yet, but you are meeting soulmates and karmics who will help you on your way to your twin soul. In this case, follow your heart to whomever you're most interested in, while also releasing attachment. You will eventually vibrate out of a soulmate, false twin, or karmic twin through healing work, while you will never truly vibrate away from a twin soul.

JOURNALING PROMPTS

- Do you have clarity on who your twin soul is or how to figure it out? What can you do to get clarity on this, and how will it speed up your journey?

- Which of the three tools for identifying your twin soul resonate, and what were the results of your test when you completed it? Did the tests bring you peace? Why or why not?

- Which relationships from your past need a label in order to better understand them? How can labels help you better identify your twin soul and move forward with your twin soul journey?

FEELING STUCK?

- **Get clarity on your journey with the 3x3x3 Signs and Synchronicities Test.** Grab the

3x3x3 Signs and Synchronicities Test in print-able format. This test can help you learn to have robust conversations with the Universe, which improves your communication with your twin soul. Get the printable at http://cardreadingqueen.com/signs-synchronicities-test

- **Discover yourself and what you desire in a twin soul.** The Twin Soul Union Core Values List is an important document that can help you stay on track on your twin soul journey. You can invest a lot of time into this and explore deeply using the printable that takes you through 10 questions that are core to who you and your twin soul are. After completing this list, you'll feel very clear on what you want in life, which will make it easier to attract your twin soul! I also share two free episodes of my Youtube channel/podcast that explain more about the core values list, called **How To Create Your Twin Soul Union Core Values List** and **10 Questions To Help You Create Your Twin Soul Union Core Values List**. Learn more about the Twin Soul Union Core Values List at http://cardreadingqueen.com/core-values-list

- **Get assurance on your twin soul's identity.** Still struggling to identify your twin soul? Grab my book, *Find Your Twin Soul: The Nine Foolproof Ways You Can Recognize and Confirm*

Your Twin Soul (Twin Soul Hearts in Union #2). You can find out more about this book at http://cardreadingqueen.com/books/

- **Figure out whether the person you are with is a twin soul, soulmate, or false/karmic twin.** Are the labels for the spiritual connections helpful to you in sorting through your persona relationships? Grab my book, *Twin Souls vs. Soulmates vs. Karmic Twins: How To Identify, Understand, and Interpret Every Spiritual Connection in Your Life To Find Harmony in Your Twin Soul Union (Twin Soul Hearts in Union #3).* You can find out more about this book at http://cardreadingqueen.com/books/

Chapter Four

THE TWIN SOUL STAGES

I f you search for "twin soul stages" in your favorite search bar, you're likely to come across the concept of twin soul separation quickly. The idea plays into the narrative of star-crossed lovers, which is often portrayed in literature and film as two individuals from opposite sides of the tracks who meet, fall in love, then are ripped apart by external forces—two competing families, one is a vampire and the other is a human, or they are simply too far apart in class with one being very wealthy and the other having nothing to his name. (Most likely, you can name at least a few movies or books that fit each of these examples!)

In spiritual truth, however, you can be with your twin without physical separation. There is always some level of the illusion of separation in your union— this is what you're healing—and physical separation could be one of those levels for you and your twin, or not. It doesn't matter either way as your journey is perfect for you and teaching you the perfect lessons in the perfect timing. In fact, if physical separation is what you fear and you don't heal through it, you'll likely manifest it for your union.

THE TWIN SOUL STAGES

I'm not the biggest fan of trying to explain this journey in stages because there's truly nothing linear about this journey. That said, since this book is about your twin soul journey, it probably makes sense to offer some sort of road map. In this chapter, I've laid out the stages to get to your twin soul union—but beware! Don't get attached to what stage you're at, don't try to skip ahead of where you are, don't beat yourself up for where you are, don't try to control your journey to get to your destination faster, and don't overestimate how much you've healed, as there is always more and we tend to heal in a spiral rather than a line.

Instead, come to this roadmap from a place of curiosity and non-attachment. See what it brings up for you. See where your own twin soul story fits... and where it doesn't... and where it doesn't need to. Use this roadmap to ease any surprise, anxiety, or fear of the unknown that might be holding you back from taking the next step on your journey. Use this roadmap only if it makes you feel good! There is nothing to fear on this journey.

THE EARLY STAGES OF TWIN SOUL UNION

You may experience the early stages of twin soul union with every potential twin soul you meet, including catalysts, false twins, and karmic twins. Please know that finding yourself in these early stages (or back at these early stages) does not mean you are not far along in the journey. Again, you heal in a spiral, and sometimes you are taken back to stages to better understand and master them for your highest good.

SOUL CONNECTION

The Soul Connection Stage is usually just a spark, a window into the twin soul journey. For some, it could be the catalyst for exploring twin flame and twin soul concepts.

In this stage you may feel connected to someone at the soul level, but you can't put words, feelings, or thoughts around it to explain the connection.

This person is not necessarily your twin soul, as you are simply accessing your intuition that you were meant to meet this person during this stage. This person could also be a soul family member, a soulmate, or a false or karmic twin. Over time your healing work will reveal the truth of the connection to you.

You may experience a soul connection many times in your life, and you may feel a sense of recognition because you've known this person from past lives or even experienced the same pattern you're experiencing with them in your current life.

Experiencing a soul connection is beautiful and peaceful. This person feels like home to you in some way. If you've been calling in your twin soul, it's possible that this is the person!

AWAKENING

The Awakening Stage is referring to your own awakening to a desire for your twin soul. You may not have a word for your twin soul or twin flame yet—most people don't until they've done an internet search—but you have accessed the desire in your heart, which activates this journey.

You realize your desire and begin to naturally pursue it through the Law of Attraction, as the Law of Attractio responds entirely to bringing the subconscious to the conscious and healing it.

If you are in the Awakening Stage, you have healed your separation from your desire for your perfect romantic mate. This is one of the early steps that leads you to your twin soul journey.

SEEKING

The Seeking Stage may have you looking for answers around your new soul connection, your new awakened desires, or the concept of twin souls or twin flames.

It's important to seek as much information about the topic as you can and to discern what applies to you and what doesn't. Everything you seek is your own understanding of your own twin soul journey, so if it doesn't resonate, always discard it. There is nothing to fear around this as you can't ever truly discard the truth—the truth always comes back to you in a different form or in different timing.

The spiritual community can feel like the Wild West sometimes, so I encourage you to seek multiple sources to aid in your understanding of twin souls. Seeking will help you fine-tune trust in yourself.

RECOGNITION

The Recognition Stage is when you recognize this person to be your twin soul at an intuitive level. You may even check out some of my other books to confirm this. One called *Find Your Twin Soul* gives detailed instructions on nine different ways to recognize and confirm your twin soul, while the other called *Twin Soul vs. Soulmate vs. Karmic Twin* helps you identify all your spiritual connections so you can recognize your twin soul through the process of elimination.

The person may or may not be your twin soul, but in spiritual truth it doesn't even matter. You can ask your higher power for signs that this person is the next step to finding your true twin soul.

CONFIRMATION

The Confirmation Stage allows you to pursue this person as your twin flame or twin soul. You may notice yourself falling in love with the person or receiving signs and synchronicities that this is the one (or, at least, this is the next one). You can certainly confirm that there is something different, magical, cosmic, and spiritual about this person, as if you are meant to be. Destiny has brought you both to the same place and same moment in order for you to have this experience.

THE MIDDLE STAGES OF TWIN SOUL UNION

You may experience the middle stages of twin soul union for some time as this is where much of the healing happens. Remember, you are deconstructing a lifetime of societal expectations, social conditioning, wounding, and false beliefs, so give yourself compassion during this time.

The greatest choice you can make when in the

middle stages is to have patience. That sentence even may be triggering to you—it's one of the blocks you are meant to heal during these stages—but your choice is a gift of self-love. The middle stages do not need to take much time, but there is a divine order to them that unfolds perfectly according to what you and your higher power choose to co-create.

Some unions spend years in these stages, while others choose to heal them gently through long friendships or acquaintanceships before stepping into romance. Still others choose to physically separate and heal them with soulmates, false twins, and karmic twins in order to preserve the love and warm feelings in the union. No option is easier or more preferable than another, in my observation; each has its upsides, downsides, and deep pains to heal. The difference in these paths is merely which story attracts you most. Trust your higher power to give you the perfect love story that your union ultimately desires.

CONTRAST

The Contrast Stage is when you get triggered by your twin soul. This can happen not long after you come together in close intimacy and proximity and are awakened to the journey with each other. Your twin soul is going to show you all your deepest and darkest wounds, and you are unlikely to unite and hold your relationship together permanently until you have healed through those wounds.

Healing wounds does not have to be difficult when you have the tools with which to feel your pain and heal it permanently. I share my own tools throughout this book, but specifically in chapters 9, 10, and 11 of this book.

As you spend time with your twin, you may experience Tower Moments, Runner and Chaser Moments, and Dark Nights of the Soul. You may also experience the masculine and feminine energies within your union, and specifically the pattern of the masculine focusing on self, while the feminine focuses on the union. All of these experiences are ultimately rooted in illusion, but it's okay to feel every feeling and upset that arises for you during these experiences, as it's the upset that leads you to greater peace.

SEPARATION

The Separation Stage is what you are healing at every step on the journey. You will experience separation (not necessarily physical, but separation of some sort) because that is literally what this journey is. Separation is the illusion, created by wounding and false beliefs. You are to break through the illusion of separation by uncovering every place that you feel separation from your higher power and your twin soul, and choosing union there instead.

Separation is not something to fear at all. Until

you are a master at union and have attained every desire in your heart, you are always healing separation from something. In spiritual truth, revealing any separation between you and your twin is a gift because within this book, you have the tools to heal it. Every time I heal a separation between my twin and me, we end up going deeper into our love, and our relationship becomes better than I could have dreamed.

BELIEF

The Belief Stage is a deeper experience of twin souls in your personal life. The literature on twin souls matches your reality, personal story, and experience. As a result, you choose to commit to the twin soul journey and see it through to the end, until you are in union with your twin soul.

PRACTICE

The Practice Stage is turning your belief of the twin soul journey into a habit. It means learning the tools necessary to heal yourself and your union. The twin soul work is truly a way of life and a way to ascend yourself, your twin soul union, and the planet. It's not a journey of getting together with a person, but rather a journey of going deeper with your higher power, who is your source for everything.

I share my own tools for practicing ascension in

your daily life throughout this book and the rest of my *Twin Soul Hearts in Union* series, but I encourage you to seek out other spiritual tools that may further assist you in the healing process.

As you heal, you change your vibration and see results in yourself, your twin soul, and your union.

Healing is not a one-time thing, any more than eating right and exercising is a one-time thing. Healing is a transformation, an embodiment, a practice that you become and lean into more and more with each passing day.

THE ADVANCED STAGES OF TWIN SOUL UNION

The longer you are on this journey, the more you truly understand the purpose of both ascension and uniting with your twin. Your twin soul can be the hook that opens you to the journey, but your journey is truly about you feeling better, going after your desires, and experiencing the joy, peace, and love you deserve and have always wanted.

Your twin soul is a part of this, but so is everything else. In spiritual truth, your twin soul is a foundational piece upon which you can build your dream life—but it's not the only one. In these stages, you are aligning to your true self, which attracts all these foundational pieces into your reality. As you receive one, the others easily come toward you as well, because each foundational piece paves the way for the rest to fall into place. That means that you can pursue your twin soul union just as easily by working on your perfect home of divine purpose as you can by pursuing your twin directly.

There is no need to strive to reach the Advanced Stages outlined below. These stages will find you when you have completed enough of your healing work, so stay consistent and keep going. In spiritual truth, you will reach these stages and the ones beyond them when you are already thriving in your relationship with your higher power and with life.

EXPANSION

The Expansion Stage is when you see and understand how every relationship you have with everyone and everything is simply a reflection of your relationship with your higher power. This is why understanding the concept of the Twin Soul Trinity that I lay out in Chapters 5-8 is going to help you advance on your twin soul journey quickly.

UNLOCKING

The Unlocking Stage opens your heart to your higher power and all that comes with the relationship, including faith, trust, hope, and love. You become powerful and connected to above (in spiritual truth you always were, but just lived under the illusion of poverty and powerlessness). You understand that your choice is how you co-create and partner with your higher power, and you realize that learning to co-create and partner with your higher power easily draws your twin soul toward you.

As you unlock your heart, you also unlock your truest and deepest heart's desires. Most of our supposed desires are chosen through ego, which is often rooted in societal and social expectations. What do you really desire at your core, though? You find it as you uncover yourself more deeply, and you move toward it through your willingness to co-create with your higher power.

DISCERNMENT

The Discernment Stage helps you take notice of the people and things that match your ideal and truest vibration, and the ones that don't. You can now tell the difference through fine-tuned discernment that is rooted not in ego, but in uncovering your truest self and truest vibration at the core. As you learn and express who you are more deeply, your permanent and ideal life will begin to manifest around you.

THE EXPERT STAGES OF TWIN SOUL UNION

When you don't need your twin, but rather simply

want your twin and are willing to do the work until you unite and beyond, this is when you'll reach the Expert Stages of the journey.

For myself, I felt a shift away from doing the healing work as part of a twin soul journey or to "get" something (as most of us want to get our twin soul in some way, which only repels them). I also felt an ongoing and permanent sense of peace that was hard to shake, and an inner union of balance in realizing that I don't need anything to happen in any time frame.

This is when the journey becomes fun and playful, as you know you would continue to do your inner work regardless of whether your twin soul came to you in the way you expect. Once you've released neediness and codependency, you are clear to focus wholeheartedly on playful desire. Your desires have no choice but to magnetize toward you.

RELEASE

The Release Stage invites you to release your attachment to the person, to the path, and to the dichotomies and duality world we currently live in. As you release, you sink into a natural state of flow and receiving, which attracts your twin soul right to you. Through releasing, you realize that the twin soul journey is a path to ascension and very much a solo endeavor—and that it always has been. You understand that the way to recognize your twin soul is to recognize yourself, that the way to unite with your twin soul is to unite with yourself, and that the way to complete the work is to accept that the work is never done but you are and always have been complete within and can handle anything life throws your way.

You release who you are, who they are, who you are together, and how it all plays out. This creates the space within which it can unfold beautifully just as your heart desires.

PEACE, LOVE, AND JOY

The Peace, Love, and Joy Stage teaches you that you can always choose peace, love, or joy at any time, regardless of what your twin or anyone else in the world is doing. Nothing can take away your peace, love, or joy because you no longer tolerate that in your reality. This is not achieved through ignoring your blocks or upsets, but rather through completing the healing on every upset that comes up.

You also realize that your twin is attracted to you most when you remain in your peace, in your love, and in your joy on your own. Your twin soul can tell this at the energetic level—there is no way to cheat on this! It must be felt.

You fully understand that your twin soul can't give you anything that you can't give yourself because the two of you are one and make the same core choices at every turn.

UNION

The Union Stage shows you that you can come into union with anything and anyone you desire and recognize all at the energetic level rather than the physical level. You've become a master manifestor who can heal separation from all true desires.

You may spend time in the Union Stage achieving inner union within yourself, or reuniting with your twin in the physical.

DIVINE PURPOSE, HOME, HEALTH AND WEALTH

The Divine Purpose, Home, Health and Wealth Stage is about stepping into your dreams beyond your union and aligning to everything that is truly meant for you, including your higher power's purpose for you. If you are curious what is truly meant for you, you must only get to know yourself better, unveil the truest desires of your heart, and commit to receiving only the things that are truly meant for you (and releasing anything that is not).

Union is just one foundational block in your life, with Purpose, Home, Health, and Wealth being several other major ones. You can start your life or divine purpose at any time, and many on the twin soul journey find that starting this is one way to bring their twin soul closer to them in the physical. You can also begin building the home life of your dreams, which includes your house, car, possessions, and family members. Perhaps you already have children or pets, or perhaps you've already created a loving space to welcome in your union. Remember that it's also okay to start where you are, and that your purpose, home, and romantic union are always upgradable because you can always go deeper into them.

If you are unsure of how to start, simply love what's right in front of you as much as you possibly can. For example, although we do not currently live in our dream home, and although we do not have the property acreage we desire, we are still remodeling our outdoor space because in order to get to the next house, we have to fully love the home we are in already. You can do the same with a job or even with a partner if you are not ready to fully release a relationship.

Continue to do your healing work and align with your higher power. Every aspect of your dreams can be fulfilled calmly and pleasantly, you just need to heal the separation that is holding you back from experiencing it in your reality.

THE MASTERY STAGES OF TWIN SOUL UNION

I know little about the Mastery Stages of this journey as I have not come anywhere near achieving them for myself, nor have I met anyone who has achieved them for themselves. I can only imagine what these stages might look like as an outsider. As such, this section remains incomplete until I can observe, feel and ground into the energy of twin soul mastery.

COMPLETE UNION

The Complete Union Stage means that you no longer have upsets as you've healed control, betrayal, shame, injustice, abandonment, and rejection in every aspect of your life. This shows up in your relationships with other people, but also with other objects, living creatures (including pets, food, and nature) and concepts (including money, politics, religion).

COMPLETE CONTENTMENT

The Complete Contentment Stage means that you no longer have unmet desires because you receive everything you desire every day. This is not achieved through suppressing your true desires, but rather through attaining a heavenly state on earth. In heaven, there are no desires as everything can be instantly manifested!

COMPLETE PURPOSE

The Complete Purpose Stage means that you are

living, breathing, and fulfilling your purpose for being on this planet in every day and even in every minute. You are consistently and constantly in communication with your higher power in everything you do and you only co-create in love. You radiate your truest self and your purest love to everything and everyone you meet, and you solely serve yourself, your twin soul, and your higher power in every choice you make. Your life around you (your wealth, health, and home) supports your ability to give to the world.

JOURNALING PROMPTS

- Which grouping of stages are you at?

- How can you go deeper into your current stage?

- How can you get to your next stage?

Chapter Five

THE TWIN SOUL TRINITY

A t age 22, I sat next to my soon-to-be husband, across from our local priest. Up until that point, our Catholic marriage counseling had been fairly ho hum and standard, meeting all the expectations I had grown up with in a devoutly Catholic household.

Get on with it, I thought. I knew how the Catholic church worked and all I wanted to do was get married in it.

"When you are married in the Catholic church," the priest said, "it is not just a marriage between two people. It is actually a sacred union between three."

He held his pointer finger up like it was a pencil. "You, your spouse, and God." As he said each one, he poked the space in front of him three times, forming an invisible triangle in the air.

My scattered, half-daydreaming thoughts coalesced to the space in front of him, focusing in on the scene he was drawing in front of us. In all my years of Catholic schooling and studies, I had never heard of this sacred union.

"And as you grow toward God in the Catholic faith," he continued, "you also grow toward your spouse, and that's how you make your marriage last for eternity."

I felt my skin tingle. I desperately wanted to make my marriage last, and there were parts of me that worried it wouldn't.

"That's what I want," I said out loud, excitedly.

At that moment, all of my fears about getting married vanished. Something in my heart was deeply drawn to the simple concept this priest had just laid out, and I knew that it was the thing missing in my world. It was the answer and the way in which I was going to live my life and make things perfect and stay fulfilled, until my dying day.

I wanted to grow closer to God and thus to my spouse. I wanted eternal love built on the foundation of God. Really, I wanted *God*, period.

WHAT IS THE TWIN SOUL TRINITY?

Without realizing it, I had stumbled on a key concept of the twin soul journey, the Twin Soul Trinity. At the time, I had no words for it, and no realization that every major religion in the world believed in this sacred connection between masculine, feminine, and their higher power—God, the Universe, Source, Spirit, your Creator, Mother Nature, or life itself.

Now that I understand the concept better, I can explain what it means and how it fits in the context of your twin soul journey.

THE TWIN SOUL TRINITY

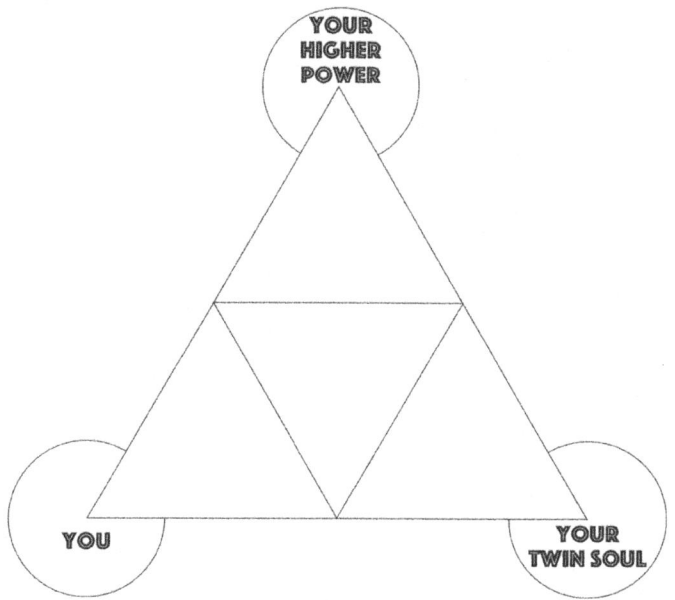

The Twin Soul Trinity is the connection between you, your higher power, and your twin soul. The outer triangle describes the relationships between the three of you, while the inner triangle describes the connections between these three relationships.

The outer triangle is equilateral, meaning that all three sides are the exact same length, and will remain equilateral.

Thus, as you grow closer to your higher power, the triangle just gets smaller until it reaches a single point at its center. That means that as you grow closer to your higher power, you also grow closer to your twin soul.

THE TWIN SOUL TRINITY

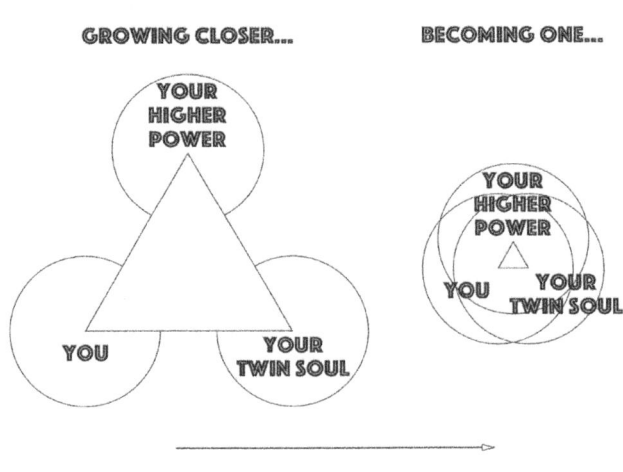

AS YOU HEAL WITH YOUR HIGHER POWER, YOU GROW CLOSER TO YOUR TWIN SOUL

Your ascension journey is healing the separation between you and your higher power in every area of your life. As you do this, it affects your twin soul (and anything else you desire) and brings that to you as well. This happens on every level, including the physical.

Eventually, if you have healed every aspect of separation between you and your higher power, you and your twin soul will converge into a Complete Union as described in the chapter on Twin Soul Stages. To do this would be to attain an extremely high and rare level of spiritual mastery, but don't get caught up in this definition of success.

You do not have to heal every aspect of separation to unite with your twin soul in the physical—not even close. If that were the case, no one would be in a physical relationship with their twin soul. The reason you don't have to heal to this level is because physical reunion is truly only a small point of separation and all the ways you can feel separated from your higher power or your twin soul.

This Twin Soul Trinity visualization is powerful because it explains and guides how twin souls truly work. I'll spend the next several chapters discussing each of the three main relationships—you and your higher power, you and your twin soul, and your twin soul and your higher power—and how they work together to bring you total fulfillment in your romantic life and relationship.

The Twin Soul Trinity promises:

- That you have a twin soul and a shared higher power

- That you can manifest all of your true desires in your heart through your relationship with your higher power, including your twin soul

- That your relationship with your higher power is reflected in your twin soul and brings your twin soul to you without you having to focus on the 3D relationship with your twin soul

- That you are your twin soul are tapping into a shared consciousness, sometimes described as you and your twin soul being one, which means that the two of you can never truly leave each other

- That your twin soul grows toward your higher power as you grow toward your higher power and in the same ways that you grow toward your higher power, which means that you will never want to leave each other, and will continue to challenge and excite each other with no compromise, eternally

This is a lot to promise and we will be unpacking the Twin Soul Trinity and the visualizations that I've shared here over the next several chapters.

BELIEVING IN A HIGHER POWER

For now, you may be wondering, *higher power? But I just want [insert your suspected twin soul's name here]. I didn't sign up for all this God talk or a higher pow-*

er to be involved.

I get it. I spent years as an atheist, rejecting both religion and spirituality in favor of cold, hard facts and science.

A lot of people want to believe that they can get their twin soul or "one," "person," love of their life, marital partner, soulmate, or whatever else they want to call it by circumventing any sort of spiritual work.

I don't exactly blame them. It is more fun to focus on your twin soul and the relationship you want to build with them. It is not fun to be cut off from them or unable to control them and instead have to focus on yourself or your relationship with your higher power. And then, it is even more disheartening to try the spiritual work and not see immediate results in the physical.

At the same time, the Twin Soul Trinity is the foundation of how your relationship with your twin soul works. To ignore this is to push your twin soul away and stay stuck in the energetic cycle of anger, frustration, control, scarcity, poverty, and resentment. You simply aren't going to get your twin soul by bypassing your higher power.

This is not me being difficult or right; instead, I'm recognizing the truth and sharing it with as many people as possible in order to assist everyone on the planet in reuniting with the desires in their hearts. Feel free to test this if it's where you are at; there is no judgment from me. I tested trying to cajole, convince, and manipulate my partners into what I wanted for nearly a decade before I accepted the truth of the Twin Soul Trinity. Once I accepted it and did my inner work, my relationship and life became deeply peaceful and only becomes more and more peaceful every day.

Perhaps you have tested other ways to get your romantic needs met and have come to the concept of twin souls, but you would really like some proof that they actually exist, beyond me or anyone else simply saying so? You're in luck. In the next several chapters, I share the step-by-step proof I used to understand exactly how twin souls really work. As a former computer science and physics major, I have a background in symbolic logic and have used that background to build a strong case for the Twin Soul Trinity existing and working as I described above. At the time of this writing, there is no one else who has presented the truth of twin souls in a linear and logical proof format.

GOING DEEPER WITH THE TWIN SOUL TRINITY

After our marital counseling session with the Catholic priest, I chatted incessantly with my fiancé about this concept of twin souls, though I didn't know that's what I was talking about at the time. He seemed interested in it, as he too wanted our marriage to last. From that moment on, we were devout in our efforts to attend church, complete our counseling and classes, and prepare for our wedding day.

Yet, shortly after the rings had been exchanged, I found myself asking my now husband when we were going back to church.

"Church?" he asked.

"Yeah," I said nervously. "We just got married in the Catholic church. Don't you want to keep attending?"

He laughed. "Oh, we just did that so they would let us get married. I don't actually believe in any of that."

My chest deflated, though I had already known the answer before I asked. To be fair, my ex-husband was not raised Catholic and considered himself a Buddhist, despite making a near-zero effort to study Buddhism beyond the meme level, nor demonstrating any semblance of being on an enlightenment path. I knew going into the marriage that he was willing to play ball with the Catholic faith to give me the wedding day I wanted, and I myself had said I was fine if afterward we released Catholicism, at least until we had children.

There was a small part of me, however, that had hoped that his seeming interest in church had grown from sincerity and was not entirely an act. When I spoke to him about growing closer to God, he always agreed that he wanted it, right up the moment after he had taken what he really wanted: me. This became a pattern between us: him lying and manipulating to get what he wanted, and me trying to get my higher power to change his heart and move him to make new decisions that aligned to mine.

Although I didn't know with certainty in that moment that we would get divorced, it was one of many moments that would eventually reveal my ex-husband to be a karmic twin, sent by my higher power to teach me some much-needed lessons in discernment around what true love actually felt like. Hint: It was not what my ex was giving me. But what was it?

The Twin Soul Trinity makes a number of promises about love:

- That we are perfect, enough, and worthy of the love we desire

- That we are at the perfect and most efficient place to receive the lessons we need to heal into the love we desire

- That life can only get better as we heal and grow, even if we make mistakes on the way

- That our higher power has ZERO desire to see us suffer, and is instead a supporting force

- That we don't need to do anything more than align to our design (our true desires) to receive all the good that already belongs to us

Again, this is a lot to promise. I have noticed that most people have resistance to at least one of these bullet points, but usually more. And that's okay. Societal beliefs around religion, science, and "the way things work" have provided most of us with a distorted view of love. I'm sharing the Twin Soul Trinity to help shift that distorted view to divine, so we can all receive the deep and true love that we want and deserve, instead of the empty and ephemeral love that society would like us to settle for.

HOW RELIGION HAS DISTORTED THE TWIN SOUL TRINITY (AND THUS, OUR VIEW OF HOW LOVE AND MARRIAGE WORKS)

After my ex-husband stopped going to church with me, I think I gave up on love. I doubt I am alone in the number of people who have lost their faith through a failed marriage. At the time, I felt stuck in my marriage and the people pleaser in me was willing to put up with just about anything to make it work. I didn't have hope to have a real relationship with God, because what was the point? Without my husband on board, I felt it would only work against my goal of keeping my marriage together.

Yet, this conversation with the priest stuck in my mind for many years until I stumbled on the concept of twin souls. Looking back, I now see that religion has misunderstood and distorted the concept of marriage in a number of ways. For example, you can't take any two random people and put them in a "sacred marriage" and tell them that as they grow toward God they'll grow toward each other. That doesn't actually work. If two random people are both growing toward God, they will only also grow toward the things and people that align to their soul design, like their twin soul.

It is not the sacred marriage rituals that bind these two people together; that is just control. And religious entities have used this concept to pair off and control men and women for centuries. Many religions, particularly those that have been around for centuries, are largely centered around labeling things good or bad, which is rooted in control, strict black and white ruling, and an outdated discipline/reward style of building a relationship.

Religion still teaches a distorted parent/child relationship to a higher power that is rooted in separation—primarily control, shame, rejection. For example, religion will teach you that if you don't obey God, he will smite or punish you in some way.

This is simply not the way God works, though. Your higher power can only recognize union, love, peace, and joy and can only engage and interact with you from these places.

HOW LACK OF RELIGION HAS DISTORTED THE TWIN SOUL TRINITY (AND THUS, OUR VIEW OF HOW LOVE AND MARRIAGE WORKS)

And what about atheism? Atheism, while not a religion, is a belief system largely rooted in rejecting meaning, magic, and connection to a creator or higher power. Atheism favors and teaches coincidence, randomness, and abandonment by a creator or higher power.

This is another distorted parent/child relationship to a higher power that is rooted in separation—primarily abandonment, injustice, and betrayal. Furthermore, nihilism is depressing and eventually begs the question, "why am I still here?"

It is a higher power and only a higher power that can pair off two people, and not through marriage at all. You don't get into marriage and then build the relationship with your higher power to hold it together. Instead, you build your relationship with your higher power and then your eternal partner (who you are spiritually married to already) comes into your reality.

This is what the Twin Soul Trinity promises. And when I think back to why I felt so attracted to what the priest had described, I realized what I really wanted was:

- Belief that my relationship could only get better and more loving as we worked on it

- A system or rule to use to face any challenge that came up in my relationship

- The safety and security and control of never being abandoned by the person I loved

What I truly desired was to know that love was real and that nothing outside of me could harm my love... not even my partner. He could not abandon me, reject me, or betray me in a way that split us up.

Yet, at 22 years old, I was still looking outside of myself for so much: specifically, my safety, my security, and my sovereignty.

Although I had the concept of the Twin Soul Trinity, and although I wanted it with every cell in my body, I was approaching it through ego and control:

- Thinking I could choose my twin soul through marriage

- Thinking I could do the healing work to keep a specific person around

- Thinking I could build a relationship with God in order to secure his abundance and good favor

We crave for the Twin Soul Trinity to be real because it supports our belief and understanding that nothing can be threatened. We crave our twin soul for the same reason. We want permanent love that we know is not going to end through growing apart, cheating, divorce, or death. We also want a sense of destiny when it comes to love because we want to believe that we are with the perfect person, in the perfect space and time, and that there is no greater happiness out there to be had.

I have found that everything I just mentioned needs to be healed within before we get our twin soul—not after.

HOW SCIENCE HAS DISTORTED THE TWIN SOUL TRINITY (AND THUS, OUR VIEW OF HOW LOVE AND MARRIAGE WORKS)

Science, like religion, also largely supports the concept of the Twin Soul Trinity, this time from the healing perspective.

The Twin Soul Trinity desires to take you back to the point of creation, your higher power, to heal any trauma or wounding that is holding you back from receiving your desires.

Psychology also attempts to take you back to your point of creation, but because it is a secular approach, it points you to your parents as your point of creation.

There is plenty of psychology dedicated to childhood wounding, the mother wound, the father wound, and other similar concepts. And yet, you can do a ton of work on these wounds, and while it certainly does seem to help many people, most still don't find complete peace or fully move past the old, ingrained patterns.

In the distorted implementation of this work, adults are encouraged to over-villainize or over-blame their parents for the things in their life that they are unhappy with. They may cut off those same parents to stop the pain without truly healing what is underneath it. They may continue to give away their power to their past experiences with their parents without realizing that they do not have to live with trauma and can choose to move forward in peace at any time.

Psychology, like religion, is evolving to better understand this. The research takes you back close to the point of creation, which is moderately effective and can produce many results; however, this is not the true point of creation.

The Twin Soul Trinity expands on what psychologists understand and agree upon by pointing to the true point of creation—your creator and higher power. Psychology can offer to cut the root of your wounding down to the ground. This can feel like great progress, but as every gardener knows, a tree cut down to ground level will only grow back within weeks or months.

The Twin Soul Trinity, on the other hand, can

help you uproot the tree from the ground.

PROOF OF THE TWIN SOUL TRINITY

You likely understand your relationship to your twin soul as a physical one between two humans. I've also explained what you can expect from your relationship to your higher power, and how society has given you distorted modeling of this relationship through how the parent/child relationship is taught in both religion and science.

The next several chapters explain the Twin Soul Trinity and each of its relationships step-by-step through the Universal Laws that form the foundation of the New Thought/New Age spiritual movements that have gained widespread acceptance over the last 100-150 years.

I've chosen to do this because what I'm about to lay out for you in the coming chapters was incredibly helpful to me in discerning which twin soul concepts held truth, and which ones didn't.

Additionally, there is a large library of books that cover all twelve of the Universal Laws that are a part of the New Thought/New Age movements. Each law can be independently tested and there are hundreds of books that will help you test your own understanding and reality. I cannot prove to you that these laws exist, or that they are the way the world works. Only you can discover that for yourself. I've provided some exercises at the end of each chapter so you can seek the truth for yourself, along with other books that will direct you to New Thought/New Age material on this.

Finally, if I had to label my own understanding of spirituality, I would consider myself New Age. I have tested all of the twelve Universal Laws for myself and have built my understanding of twin souls on the previous thought that has come before me, as all scientists should do. I desired and was called to break down the Twin Soul Trinity into the step-by-step foundational building blocks so that the concepts could be isolated and tested by each of you as well. I hope you'll accept my invitation to test the Twin Soul Trinity for yourself and see what you believe. It is critical to the success of your journey toward your twin soul.

JOURNALING PROMPTS

- Does the Twin Soul Trinity concept resonate with you? Why or why not?

- How do you feel about a sacred union of three? Do you believe in a higher power or the necessity of working with a higher power to grow closer to your twin soul?

- What came up for you when I spoke about how

religion has distorted the twin soul union?

- What came up for you when I spoke about how science has distorted the twin soul union?

FEELING STUCK?

- **Learn more about the Twin Soul Trinity.** I've put together a page of resources that can take you deeper into these concepts, beyond the content of this book. Listen, watch, and read at http://cardreadingqueen.com/twin-soul-trinity/

Chapter Six

TWIN SOULS AND THE LAW OF ATTRACTION

I n 2013 I was 29 years old, newly divorced, with about eight dollars in my bank account. I had long since left my 6-figure corporate career, maxed out my credit cards, gotten behind on payments, and moved in with my boyfriend, to whom I was supposed to be paying rent. I was trying to make writing work as a career, but I couldn't figure it out or ground into it, even though I knew it was my divine purpose.

I didn't have much faith in a higher power anymore after shunning my religious upbringing, so I instead started considering other means of making money and eventually stumbled on the Law of Attraction.

One of the exercises to test the idea that money was everywhere was to go outside and pay attention to the ground, where I would easily find abandoned pennies that I could claim as my own.

I felt skeptical. I lived in downtown Chicago where hundreds of people traversed a single block over the course of just a few hours. What was the likelihood that I would find money on the ground, when so many others were walking right by it too? But I had a small dog who needed regular bathroom breaks, so I decided to use that time to learn about manifesting money on the street.

To my surprise, I found pennies almost immediately! *Hmm*, I thought curiously.

The exercise then suggests that you continue upgrading your ask, from pennies to nickels, from nickels to quarters, and so on. I again felt skeptical—I had definitely been keeping my eyes on the ground, and wouldn't I have noticed silver coins more easily than pennies?

Once again, I was proven wrong. As soon as I reset my intentions, I began finding nickels and pennies and sometimes even dimes, though those were harder to spot. In fact, I frequently found a handful of coins near each other, as if someone had dropped several in a row. Over time I started finding quarters, usually in groupings but sometimes on their own.

I noticed that not only could I find money, but I could also see my wounding and blocks around receiving money. One time I found 52 cents in a grassy section of a park. A woman nearby smiled at me as if it were hers, just as I was putting it in my pocket.

She didn't say anything, but I think she expected me to ask if it were hers. I hadn't seen her near that spot to have dropped it, so I didn't offer it to her. Several years later, I found a 5-dollar bill on the ground. A large man approached me and claimed that he had dropped it. Not wanting to start an argument or jeopardize my safety, I released the money to him and walked away. I still haven't quite healed that piece of the manifestation!

I came to manifestation because I had a physical need and desire for money. This led me to study the Law of Attraction and the Universe. I tested these concepts for many years and found them useful to not only manifest money, but also things, including new places to live and new job opportunities. But I never considered trying to manifest a boyfriend or a new way of being in my relationships until I read something profound on a blog called the Twin Flame Tribe. To paraphrase, it said something like, "you've gotta get over your issues and call the Universe what it is: God."

It occurred to me then that all along, my higher power had been trying to reach me through the concepts of manifestation. He had once been in communication with me through religion, but I had cut off that avenue. It was almost like I had blocked him on Facebook, so now he had to message me on Instagram.

I also realized that manifesting money was the same thing as manifesting your twin soul. The Law of Attraction applies to both. My higher power had been training me to manifest my twin soul all along!

THE LAW OF ATTRACTION

You've probably heard of the Law of Attraction, which is why it's a great place to start in unpacking the Twin Soul Trinity. Many will tell you that twin souls exist due to the Law of Attraction, but this is only part of the answer. We'll get to rest in due time.

The Law of Attraction is part of the New Thought/New Age movement, which has only been around since the late 19th century. It is a unionist principle that relies on the belief that you only have one higher power and your higher power does not desire you to suffer, nor does he/she/it cause you suffering. Your higher power only loves you, and even when a situation looks bad on the surface, you can see through this illusion to find how the situation has been for your highest good.

Another important belief under the Law of Attraction is that you are enough, deserving, and worthy of love by your higher power, and that you will receive everything you desire if you change your vibration to better align to it. Earth is a smorgasbord of love, but most people are out of alignment with love and thus can't experience it as their higher power intended.

Many believe the Law of Attraction means that

you can create anything you desire, but I have a different and evolved take on it. I agree that only love is real, and that everything else is an illusion. I agree that my higher power can only love me for my highest good. I agree that my higher power has no desire to see me suffer and thus the more I align to him, the greater my abundance unfolds throughout my life.

To take this deeper, though, I also believe that love is not alignment to desire, at least not completely. Love is alignment to the truth. You cannot attract anything or anyone through the Law of Attraction. You can only attract those things and people that are in alignment with your truth.

This means that in order for the Law of Attraction to work, you have to understand and come into alignment with your truth. I explain this more deeply later in this chapter.

There is a shadow side to the Law of Attraction that many people prefer to ignore or skim over. That truth is that everything and everyone around you is a mirror, perfectly reflecting back to you your inner state. If you see something you don't like in your reality, it is a symbol of a feeling or thought that's out of alignment within you. You can use the Law of Attraction to change this and get back into alignment.

There's a lot of confusion about what twin souls are and how they work, and almost all of that confusion is tied back to a misunderstanding of how the Law of Attraction works. So let's clear that up!

THE LAW OF ATTRACTION WHEN IT COMES TO TWIN SOULS

Some people believe that the Law of Attraction means you can get more money by opening yourself to more opportunities. Others believe that the Law of Attraction means you get more money by sticking to your guns and requesting it as specifically as possible. I believe a third choice: that the Law of Attraction means you get more money and attain wealth permanently only by aligning to your divine purpose.

Applying this to romance, some people believe that the Law of Attraction means you can get more love by opening yourself to more opportunities, while others believe the Law of Attraction means you get more love by focusing on a very specific person. I believe that you must align to your divine romance. This journey is not about a person and is not about choosing who you are. It's about surrendering to the truth of who you are. Everything else is control.

Breaking this down:

- Your twin soul journey is a journey to find and love yourself as you truly are

- You are neither good nor bad; neither is your twin soul; you are both perfect as you are and perfect for each other

- The way to receive love is to be in alignment

to your soul's truth

- You can only truly attract your twin soul because you can only attract what is meant for you; every other romantic partner will eventually vibrate out of your reality

I'll be exploring these statements and themes throughout the rest of this chapter.

WHAT IS THE TWIN SOUL MIRROR?

The twin soul mirror is nothing more than the mirror of the Law of Attraction, which states that what you experience in your reality is a representation or function of your relationship to your higher power.

On the Twin Soul Trinity, the relationship between you and your higher power is represented by the Law of Attraction, the first Universal Law we are covering. When you are in union with your higher power, you easily experience love in your reality through attracting beauty, abundance, peace, joy, and love. When you are not in union with your higher power, or when you are in separation with your higher power, you experience parts of your reality in states of suffering, sadness, depression, fear, ego, poverty, scarcity, control, injustice, betrayal, abandonment, shame, and rejection. This is nothing to be ashamed of—it's a part of the human experience. And as the Law of Attraction states, you can heal this by getting into alignment with that which you truly desire... or in this case, getting into alignment with your higher power. It's the same thing.

THE TWIN SOUL TRINITY

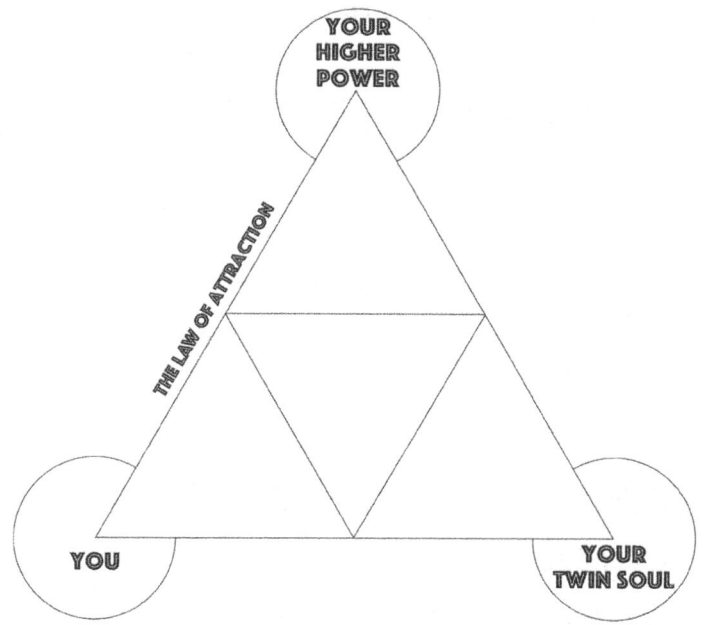

What does this have to do with your twin soul, and how does it relate to the twin soul mirror?

Your twin soul is a perfect mirror because they share the same soul DNA as you. They are the truest expression of the romantic love you desire, which means that they will love you perfectly into the person you truly desire to be.

Others in your life will offer you degrees of imperfect mirroring. Your soul family can also offer you a strong mirror, as can a soulmate, as can a karmic twin. The degree to which someone can mirror you depends largely on how close you are to them and what your wounding is.

This is no different than your dream home being a perfect mirror, while other homes leading up to that will be degrees of imperfect mirror. A cardboard box as a home is likely going to be a terrible mirror as you will vibrate out of it too easily (or never be able to vibrate into it to begin with). A home that you never enter is likely going to be a terrible mirror as you never interact with it. But a home that's very similar to your dream home would be a strong mirror as it will show you many of the same triggers that you could get with your dream home.

EVERYTHING IS NEUTRAL— NEITHER GOOD NOR BAD IN SPIRITUAL TRUTH

You may wonder, if the Law of Attraction describes how the relationship between my higher power and me works, and if I can only manifest things I truly desire, that are truly mine and meant for me permanently, then why are there things like lack and scarcity in the world? Doesn't everyone desire to drive a fancy car, live in a fancy house, or have a million dollars? Yet, there is a set amount of fancy houses and cars in the world.

And what about that job I wanted, that went to my coworker? There was only one job and we both wanted it. But she got it. Does that mean she wanted it more? Is she better than me? What's the deal?

The Law of Attraction only brings things to you when they already belong to you and are intended for you. Your higher power does not see hierarchy in things like fancy houses or competitive job openings. Hierarchy is rooted in fear, ego, and control, so your higher power cannot engage with you from a place of hierarchy.

Instead, your higher power sees all things as neutral and only tries to bring you the true desires you have in your heart—the true desires that are meant for you and would make you the happiest. When you are in union with your higher power, they bring you the perfect things to give you the greatest happiness. When you are in separation with your higher power, they bring you contrast to help you release your wounding that is keeping you in separation.

Think of it like this: there are blocks shaped like stars, squares, triangles, circles, ovals, and more spread out across the floor beneath you, in all different colors. You are one of these blocks—which one?

No block is better or worse than the other, but you will resonate with one more than the rest. Choose now.

As you are looking at the blocks on the floor,

imagine that you are tasked with putting them into some sort of organization. Do you notice that some of the blocks seem to "belong" to each other more than others? How would you organize these blocks?

The physical earth that we live on is much like someone dumped a (very large) bag of these blocks onto the floor and scattered them randomly across the continents. When you choose to work with the Law of Attraction, you are choosing to reunite with all the pieces that resonate with you. If you are a purple star, this could be the other purple stars, or if you are an orange triangle, this could be the other orange triangles.

Ascension is a collective effort to put the blocks back in order with their natural matches. You sometimes hear people say that doing your healing work helps others around you ascend. A big reason why is that as you restore the order in your life, others are also inspired to restore the order in their lives. With your blocks already organized, there are fewer blocks for them to sort through to order theirs.

You, your perfect life, and your twin soul union are all unbreakable because no one can turn from a purple star to an orange triangle. You are the block you are, and you are perfectly created as your higher power designed you, and you have your perfect matches available to you, right there next to you on the floor. You only need to reveal yourself to be the block that you are so you can find and unite with your ideal and naturally matching blocks.

EVERYTHING ON EARTH IS A TOOL

War, death, disease, politics, breakups, job loss, starvation—all are situations used by our higher power as tools to help us grow spiritually. A large national or global situation is used by our higher power to help the planet ascend, while personal tragedies and problems are used to help us individually ascend at a micro-level, which supports the planet's ascension as well.

My goal in sharing this is not to be callous about the true and real suffering in the world. I'm also not condoning any spiritual bypassing of these tragedies of the world—these challenging situations are calling for our more immediate attention, and "love and lighting" them out of your conversations, thoughts, and emotions is doing more damage than good. Avoidance is not and never will be a means to permanently heal or transcend wounding. As always, if you are experiencing something you don't like in your reality, it's because it is meant for you to notice and heal. So if you continue to notice a particular cause that keeps popping up in your reality, it's because you are meant to notice and express your emotions around it. Your soul has a desire to help the planet transcend those patterns, and ignoring that desire is only moving further away from your higher power and thus, your twin soul.

On the twin soul journey, challenge in our personal world is meant to help us grow spiritually. Twin souls are always in a state of union in the spiritual realm, sometimes called the higher dimensions or the 5D. They make decisions, communicate, and connect about what they want to learn together and separately on the planet earth. In the earthly realm, sometimes called the lower dimensions or the 3D, the pieces on the ground are merely tools—situations that can be shifted around to create. The challenging situation is never truly real. It is a tool to trigger us out of our false beliefs and wounding and into love.

Our challenges come up for us in divine order, and arrive at the level of proportion needed to get our attention. The more challenging a situation feels to our human selves, the more likely the wounding around it is being accelerated into ascension. Additionally, the more intense the challenge, the more likely we've been ignoring the wounding around it, as our higher power will keep sending us bigger and bigger challenges around the same wounding until the wounding finally has our attention.

The challenges you face with your twin soul work the same way. The more challenging the experience is, the more it is calling for your attention. If you ignore the healing work you are called to do, you will keep attracting experiences that attempt to bring that wounding back to your attention. That is how people get stuck in cycles on this journey. Please don't turn to the tarot readers on Youtube to learn when the energy is going to shift, as it's within your power to shift the energy yourself!

As you commit more deeply to the twin soul journey, you may attract more "tools" to help you ascend faster. This is why experiencing a catalyst, false twin, or karmic twin will propel you toward your true twin soul and soul family faster. Many people on the twin soul journey struggle with the thought that the person they believe is their twin soul might be a false twin, but in truth, it's perfectly safe and common to experience this on the journey. These people are just "situations" to help you grow spiritually. This does not diminish them as people in any way, nor does it mean you can't have a real, important, loving, and spiritual relationship with these people. It only means that these people are not meant to remain in your life permanently. When you release the wounding that attracted you to them, and when you release your attachment to your false belief of who they are to you, they fall away quickly. It is a blessing and gift to attract these relationships into your life as they help you more quickly align to who you really are so you can unite with your true twin soul.

WHAT CAN YOU ATTRACT? (AND WHAT CAN'T YOU?)

I cannot attract famous actor Ryan Gosling as my twin soul, because he's not meant for me.

But how do I know that? How do I know that Ryan Gosling is not meant for me, and that any crush I have on him is just a projection of my love for my twin soul?

The biggest way I can discern that Ryan Gosling is not my twin soul is to notice that we are not exuding the same energy in life. He is famous, for example; I'm not. He's more attractive and has a better body than me. He's richer and more successful than me as well! We don't travel in the same circles, we don't connect on the same divine purpose, and we don't seem to desire the same things or be making the same core choices. Your twin soul is going to be you—the same as you energetically—which is why finding, correctly identifying, and confirming your twin soul is more specifically a task of revealing yourself to yourself.

The second way I can discern this is my Twin Soul Core Values List. I don't personally know what Ryan Gosling values, but I know that the things I value would conflict with his current life. For example, I want to dress in yoga pants and wear no makeup 99% of the time, I want to move to a 10-acre property in Oregon and grow vegetables, I want to keep my children's lives private, and I want to build a romantic relationship based on my higher power, God. When I look at each of the items on this list, I can trace them all the way back to my childhood and what I have always desired for my life. Anything that seems in direct contrast with what I wanted as a child—for example, dressing comfortably and functionally as opposed to how the trendy and popular girls looked in grade school—can be traced back to wounding I had then that I've since released.

As I reveal myself more deeply to myself, I notice that Ryan Gosling is not truly planted in my heart. And when I investigate this attraction more deeply, it's clear to me that I really only like his character in *The Notebook*! Specifically, I like that the character was a simple guy, a man of fewer words but deep emotions, and a carpenter. I like that he wanted to build and raise a family closer to nature. I also like that he was so dedicated to the woman he loved that he rebuilt a house based on their love and decided to live in it, with or without her—which naturally attracted her right to him, just as the twin soul journey does.

Everything I list about why I like Ryan Gosling's *The Notebook* character is also listed on my core values list: simplicity, earthiness, space, land, nature, a deep emotional connection, and most importantly, God. I have the root of my attraction to him, only to find that I'm not attracted to him at all. Instead, I'm projecting the love and attraction I have for my twin soul onto him, because they share some of the same traits.

There is no depth to my attraction to Ryan Gosling, so it's safe to release all attachment to him. Anything I desired about him is safely wrapped up in my twin soul already. I lose nothing by releasing what is not meant for me.

WHAT DO YOU TRULY DESIRE TO ATTRACT?

What can I attract instead? I can attract any desire that is truly planted in my heart. To be truly planted in my heart means that, after I clear away all the wounding and illusion around the desire, I am attracted to it at its core. And what does that mean? To be attracted to something at its core means that when all the illusion and wounding is cleared away, I am a natural vibrational match to the desire.

This vibrational match should feel simple, inevitable and divine. In tarot, this is the easeful and contented energy of the King of Pentacles and the natural being and receiving of The Empress; in astrology, this is when two objects are aspected in a harmonious trine with one another.

Your true desires are meant for you because the source or point of creation is your higher power. Your higher power planted these desires for you as part of your soul design. You can erase them, reject them, and ignore them as long as you are willing to erase, reject, and ignore your higher power. Your design is the core of who you actually are, and your desires are the blueprint to building your purest and happiest life. Your twin soul is a foundational piece of this!

Anything that is truly planted in your heart is meant for you; you need only heal the separation between you and it. But how do you know what you truly desire to attract? How can you discern this for yourself?

The easiest way to discern this is by realizing that you don't ever want a person or thing here on planet earth. Never.

Instead, you want love and your higher power, manifested in the thing or person here on earth.

This is true of money, love, health, career, lifestyle, home, friendship, family, and more. You do not want more money; you want your higher power manifested in money. You do not want more love; you want your higher power manifested in love. You do not want a specific person to be your twin soul; you want your higher power manifested as your perfect romantic partner, which is your twin soul.

This is your permanent and everlasting love in all areas of your life, versus the false highs and short-term hits that you may be used to experiencing in life.

Have you ever gotten something you wanted, only to find it deeply empty? I used to experience this a lot, as for a long time I was always chasing the false highs. I experienced that emptiness on my wedding day with my ex-husband, when I got accepted to a prestigious graduate school at 22-years old, and when I landed my first six-figure job. I went through with my wedding in part to make others around me happy, and in part to avoid being alone, which I knew would lead me to some very challenging reckonings and confrontations about a past relationship. I applied to the fancy graduate school because I didn't feel good enough with my current educational credits; I went because I felt like it would be foolish not to claim the prestige I was being offered. I took the six-figure job because I wanted to be rich, and I thought that money in the bank was how you got there. In each of these examples, there was a simple pattern: I didn't feel worthy inside myself, so I was trying to create transformation outside of myself. I didn't like my true soul design because it wasn't prestigious, successful, people-pleasing, or wealthy, so I went down the path of ego and tried to construct and project a facade of who I wanted to be.

None of these things were truly aligned to my divine romantic love or my divine purpose in life; none of them truly made me happy.

To learn what you truly desire to attract, you have to reveal your true heart to yourself, be willing to see yourself and the truth of who you are clearly, and release any desires that are out of alignment with your true self. You can only attract what you are and what is meant for you; everything else will make you deeply unhappy or collapse easily around you. Society will teach you that becoming someone you are not at the soul level is safe, acceptable, and fulfilling. Instead, it is transient, depressing, and barren of love.

If you desire your true twin soul, you probably desire some level of permanence in your romantic partnerships. The only way to permanence is to learn to uncover your truest desires and align to your soul design. The Law of Attraction will take you the rest of the way there as you clear the separation between you and the things that were meant for you.

WHY DO PEOPLE STRUGGLE TO ATTRACT WHAT THEY WANT? (INCLUDING THEIR TWIN SOUL?)

There are many reasons that people struggle to attract their twin soul and anything else they want:

#1 - ATTEMPTING TO ATTRACT THEIR TWIN SOUL THROUGH SURFACE OR IDENTITY TRAITS

Do you hope to attract your twin soul through surface traits, like being pretty, having a fancy house, or driving a nice car?

Or perhaps you are looking a little bit deeper, and hoping to attract them through identity traits, like being kind, smart, creative, or a hard worker?

Neither works! You can be the prettiest, have the nicest car, have millions in the bank, be a genius and also genuinely nice, and it still won't be the stuff that attracts your twin soul.

Don't get me wrong—your twin soul loves all of these things about you... and at the same time, they can run far and fast from you if neither of you do the healing work. That's because the core of the attraction is at the soul level—it's a pure recognition of the truth that the two of you belong together energetically.

Consider money and how it flows through the world. There are many false beliefs about how money flows. Some believe that hard work attracts money; others believe that looks and beauty attract money. Neither is true, though if you desire to give energy to those false beliefs, you will easily find evidence that you are right!

The truth is that money can only be attracted at the soul level, too. As you clear and heal your wounds around your relationship with money, you receive more of it, to the level of your heart's desire.

The same is true for your twin soul. You must clear and heal your wounds around your relationship with love to receive it in the physical.

#2 - TAKING YOUR EGO'S PATH VERSUS TAKING YOUR SOUL'S PATH

If you are like my younger self, you may have a lot of false beliefs around love, purpose, home, and more. All of this contributes to your ego's path, which is anything that you do that is out of alignment with who you really are. This includes chasing false highs, ignoring your higher power's communication, claiming people and things that are not yours, and trying to control who you are through what you be, do, and have. Your ego's path can take you far from your true purpose, true love, true peace, and true happiness—even when it looks healthy, stable, and "normal" on the outside.

Your soul's path is the one that your higher power has laid out for you. It is perfectly aligned to your soul's design and helps you learn the lessons required to create your perfect life here on earth. You can follow your soul's path by desiring and prioritizing your relationship with your higher power. As you do this, all areas of your life must come into alignment.

#3 - ATTACHMENT TO OUTCOME

Manifestation requires you to release your attachment to outcome. What you are truly releasing is your core wound around control, which is a particularly insidious wound as it encompasses much of our fears around safety and security.

You may also be concerned about the free will of your twin soul. Free will is not real; it is a concept used to explain a person's choice to choose the illusion of separation, and thus attract chaos and distorted order into their lives.

On the flipside, you may be instead trying to manifest for your twin soul or others. This is the same wound as the one around free will, but in the opposite extreme. Both are rooted in control.

Your twin soul must choose you if you are choosing them; at the same time, you cannot manifest away their choices or relationships with other people, because you cannot manifest in another's reality. You can only manifest in your own reality, which is why healing and doing the inner work is the only way to truly attract your twin soul.

#4 - MANIFESTING FROM BLAME AND SHAME

You are unlikely to get your twin soul union through blaming and shaming yourself, your twin, others, or your higher power. Blame and shame are the antithesis of this journey. If you are finding yourself beating yourself up with phrases like, "I haven't healed enough," or "I caused this negative thing to happen to me," or "why hasn't my reality changed yet?" then you are likely trying to manifest from a place of blame.

The antidote to blame is responsibility. You can take responsibility for your reality while also having love and compassion for your past self who made choices that led to your current circumstances. By design, manifestations happen instantaneously in the spiritual realm but slowly in the earthly realm. Earth is still transcending duality and separation consciousness, and would be complete chaos if manifestations appeared quickly. Give your reality lots of time to catch up to your new vibration.

If you are struggling with blame and shame, you can eradicate these feelings completely through forgiveness and gratitude. I'll explain more about how to use these in your healing process in Chapter 10 on How To Heal and Love Yourself.

#5 - NOT FOLLOWING THE PROCESS

Your manifestation comes to you through three efforts. First, you have a thought about what you want. This is the content of your manifestation. Next, you have emotions around it, which is the energy of the manifestation. A thought without energy doesn't produce a change in your reality, and for good reason!

Finally, you have to take action on your manifestation. Your thought + emotions around the manifestation are essentially making a new choice that's different from the one you've been making to create your current reality. To create a new reality, though, you have to continue making that new choice consistently in every moment, as that's the only way to transform your vibration and attract what you really want into your reality.

WHAT ABOUT FREE WILL?

I've touched on the concept of free will throughout this book, but I wanted to fully address this misunderstood concept as it relates to the Law of Attraction.

Most people see a huge difference between what they call "free will" with money and "free will" with other humans. In their minds, money has no free will, and you cannot hurt or impose your will on money by claiming it. They believe, however, that humans do have free will and you can hurt other humans through claiming them as yours.

In truth, money and everything else on earth does have what they are calling "free will." That's because what they are calling "free will" is actually just the choice to believe in the illusion of separation consciousness. Every cent of money in the world actually does have a rightful, divine owner—this would have to be so if there is enough money for everyone, right? If you didn't have a divine level of wealth that was already yours, that satisfied all your needs perfectly, then you would ultimately be believing that your higher power wanted you to suffer, right? Furthermore, every person on the planet has inherent value, deserves all the support they truly desire, and is loved by their higher power, so this must be represented through our currency.

Every person on this planet has a divine level of wealth that supports them and their dreams perfectly. And yet, money can fall into the hands of people that it was not meant for. This happens when some claim what's not meant for them and others relinquish what is meant for them. This is the "free will" of money, which is actually just the choice of humans to separate from their divine level of wealth, taking too much or too little.

As the planet ascends, money is getting sorted and redistributed into the hands of its true owners. Everyone is meant to have a beautiful, loving, and fulfilling life. This has been prevented though by distorted patterns of control, power, and betrayal. But we are here doing this work to transcend that reality!

When people talk about free will, they are really only talking about the ability of earth to be disorganized—for purple stars to mingle with orange triangles for an extended period. In truth it's just a blip, and the energy will be returned to its rightful owner. Divine order will always eventually prevail. Thus, free will is an illusion, rooted in fear, ego, and control.

If we apply this understanding to how free will works with your twin soul, you can see that it's also an illusion.

You could choose to believe in your free will to be without your divine partner, or their free will to be without you... But this is simply buying into the illusion of separation from your divine love. You are really saying that there is no divine order to things... which means you believe in distorted order... which means that you believe that chaos and randomness rule the world... and then things get very unpleasant and disempowering.

If you instead choose to believe in divine order, then you believe that you can change your reality by uncovering the truth of what's been planted in your heart as a true desire. This is empowering. It is literally a map to your ultimate peace and happiness.

Free will doesn't truly exist. If you are choosing your divine partner, your divine partner is choosing you. You don't even need to know who they are—you can choose your divine partner by choosing to heal and stick with your twin soul journey. They have no choice but to come in as you heal. Neither you nor they can choose to not be twin souls—that's just control and ego.

JOURNALING PROMPTS

- What is your current understanding of the Law of Attraction? What are the lingering questions that you'd like to investigate more on your own?

- What connections have you made between the Law of Attraction and twin souls?

- What connections have you made between the Law of Attraction and the Twin Soul Trinity?

- Do you believe in the divine order of your desires, specifically around your twin soul? Why or why not?

- Do you believe that free will is real or an illusion? Why or why not?

FEELING STUCK?

- **Check out my additional Law of Attraction resources.** I talk a lot about the Law of Attraction on my Youtube channel and podcast, Your Twin Soul Journey. My playlist includes, Why You Can't Manifest Anyone or Anything (Six Misconceptions About the Law of Attraction). Go here: http://cardreadingqueen.com/manifestation-law-of-attraction/

- **Learn more about free will.** You can listen to, watch, and read my free content, How Twin Soul Work Handles the Concept of Free Will. Go here: http://cardreadingqueen.com/twin-flames-free-will/

Chapter Seven

TWIN SOULS AND THE LAW OF POLARITY

hen I began my twin soul journey, I was extremely confused around the polarities of the masculine and feminine. I didn't understand—we were the same consciousness, but we were opposites as well? I questioned whether I was the masculine or feminine, especially because I had spent much of my late teens and twenties trying to play ball with the guys—first as a software engineer, then as a business student, and finally at the executive level on the tech startup scene. It took me a long time to understand the concept of polarity, but I did eventually figure out what was really going on in these seemingly contradictory ideas about what the twin soul connection was.

A big part of twin soul literature is that you have a twin soul, that they look the opposite of you, but that the two of you are actually the same. The underlying thought behind the twin soul relationship is primarily based on the specific universal law called the Law of Polarity.

The Law of Polarity states that everything is dual. It suggests that if you exist, there also exists your polar opposite that helps to define you. In the case of twin souls, this specifically applies to the masculine and feminine counterparts. In the Twin Soul Trinity, the Law of Polarity describes the relationship between you and your twin soul.

The Law of Polarity also says that two things that seem to be polar opposites are actually one, as their definitions are relative to each other. This law applies to all dualities, or opposed parts of the same thing, that we find in the universe. In physics, we ask, is light a particle or a wave? Our findings thus far are that it is both; there is a wave-particle duality to it as it acts in both ways mathematically.

The classic example of something bound by the Law of Polarity is hot and cold. Something cannot be "hot" without the comparison of "cold" to help define it.

To me, what the Law of Polarity really says is that the things we initially believe are dichotomies are actually on a spectrum. Hot and cold, for example, seem like a dichotomy, but anyone who has been in a standard U.S. hotel shower has seen that the knob to turn on the hot and cold water is actually a spectrum. And in some parts of the world, 50 degrees Fahrenheit is cold, while in other parts of the world, this same exact temperature is hot. Context matters. If hot and cold are both able to describe the exact same temperature, then how can they truly be a dichotomy?

THE LAW OF POLARITY HELPS US REUNITE ARBITRARY SEPARATIONS

The Law of Polarity also allows things to ebb and flow rather than remain in a specific state. This allows for powerful transformation and expression. For example, water can transform into a liquid, solid, or gas, depending on its temperature. We use this basic substance to define boundaries within temperature on all three of the world's most used temperature scales—Fahrenheit, Celsius, and Kelvin.

But when you get down to it, the boundaries are ultimately arbitrary, just as the boundaries of water are arbitrary. Steam or vaporized water is not molecularly different from liquid water. The only true difference is that the molecules in steam are moving faster and are in a looser configuration than they are in liquid water. And the same is true of ice—it is not molecularly different from water, but the molecules have slowed down and formed a rigid configuration. While these arbitrary boundaries are extremely useful to scientists for studying the substance of water in its different phases, there is a reasonable argument to be made for not creating this separation. What if we considered a different way of categorizing water, not by its three best-known phases?

There are actually multiple additional phases of water that we know of as a collective. One is a duality phase we have only achieved in extreme conditions not found naturally on Earth. If you significantly increase the temperature and pressure of water, you can create a liquid-gas duality to it, where the fluid produced acts like both a liquid and a gas. What does this mean? Common knowledge would state that water stops being a liquid at temperatures above 212 degrees Fahrenheit, 100 degrees Celsius, and 273 degrees Kelvin. And yet, we have found scientific evidence that water resumes being a liquid of sorts at 647 degrees Kelvin (an extreme and uninhabitable scorching temperature).

In recent years, scientists have discovered many other odd transformations in water and its properties, including a new phase at 4 degrees Celsius and another at 50-60 degrees Celsius. What does this mean? Well, for starters, it means that we have lots left to uncover about water. But more importantly, it means that water is one substance that transforms in properties but not molecularity depending on the temperature and pressure. In other words, water is water is water. The phases that we know are arbitrary. There is no true separation between water as a solid, liquid, and gas. The phases of water are all just water on a spectrum.

WHY DO WE CREATE ARBITRARY SEPARATIONS?

Water is a great example of why we as humans create arbitrary separations, and why we must ultimately evolve beyond those arbitrary separations to truly understand the truth of our higher power. Originally, the separations between the three phases of water were extremely useful to scientists in understanding water. The separations were observable to the naked eye and intuitively understood by our ancestors who studied water from an urgent survivalist perspective. These separations likely helped us as a collective define water's molecular and chemical structures and properties, plus learn much more about solids, liquids, and gases that both act similarly and dissimilarly to water.

And at the same time, these separations held us back from discovering the deeper truth of water. We are still discovering this at the time of this book's writing. Scientists have many mysteries left to uncover about how water transforms, and they are only able to do so by releasing the current arbitrary separations and finding new ways to categorize water's properties.

As you can see, separation is an important part of deepening our understanding of all ideas and concepts. And it's human nature to want to dissect things to understand them.

For example, in my Core Wound Wheel, I dissect

wounding into six major categories: abandonment, betrayal, control, shame, injustice, and rejection. But in truth, they are all only one wounding: separation. The antidote is only one healing: union.

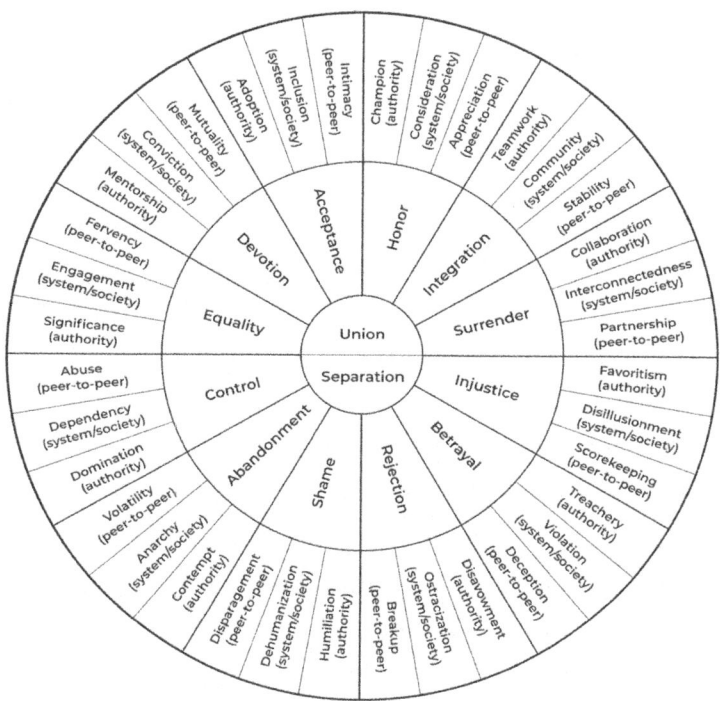

When we are stuck in the wounding of separation, however, it isn't all that helpful to focus on the vast concept of coming into union. By dissecting separation into six arbitrary categories, I'm able to explain different types of separation more easily to others. And by dissecting those categories further, I'm able to help others find all the different threads of wounding that we hold within ourselves, and heal those threads one by one, in manageable chunks.

In the same way, we create separation to explain:

- **Evolutions:** multi-ality, duality, unity

- **Transformations:** water, steam, ice, other phases

- **Ideologies:** Republicans, Democrats

- **Energies:** fear and love, masculine and feminine

People love these separations and love to choose a "side," but in truth there are no "teams" in heaven. The only thing we ever dislike about the "other side" is the distortion of it. We transcend the duality by transcending the distortion of the "otherness."

Politics is by far the easiest example of this, and many who consider themselves independent or in the middle can easily see that the largest political parties are largely the same. The thing that Republicans hate about Democrats is their own distortion of Democrat ideology, and vice-versa. I do not write this to get political or to trigger anyone, as I myself have been on both sides at one point or another in my life, and vocally passionate about my personal views in many cases! But much of my seeming disdain for either side has always been from a place of wounding and separation. I am still healing this within myself with zero shame or blame. I'm safe to be where I'm at with it and any of these other dualities or multi-alities—and so are you.

Have compassion for the arbitrary separations

you see in the world, as you'll find them everywhere now that you are aware of them. Remember that you must bring a wounding from the subconscious to the conscious to heal it. Recognizing these arbitrary separations is the first step to healing them. There is no reason to stress about seeing separation, nor to congratulate yourself for not buying into a separation where others do. There is no hierarchy in heaven! You are perfect right where you are, and you are allowed to heal at your own beautiful pace.

Separation itself is not a bad thing. Applying the Law of Polarity, separation is merely union taken apart in its pieces, the same way you might take a clock apart to understand how it works. The reason we must heal separation is because we've come to believe in the illusion, or rather, distortion of it. We've come to believe that the clock cannot be put back together again, that it is only its pieces as they are spread across the floor. We have lost the knowledge of the clock as it is meant to be, with all its parts in divine order, whole and healed and able to serve its divine purpose.

THE LAW OF POLARITY AND YOUR HIGHER POWER

Another place we have created a lot of separation is through religion and, on a larger scale, our relationship to our higher power—God, the Universe,

Source, Spirit, Mother Nature, our Creator, or life itself.

Religion is and always has been evolving right in step with the natural evolution of our world and collective consciousness. Past religions largely centered around a multi-ality toward a higher power. The Romans, Greeks, Egyptians, Pagans, and nearly all ancient cultures believed in many gods and goddesses.

It wasn't until Jesus Christ and Muhammad came along about 500 years apart that religion evolved in consciousness to a duality toward a higher power, while downgrading the gods and goddesses to saints and angels. This duality of our collective higher power reflected the duality consciousness that the collective on Earth at the time had also evolved to understand.

Many religions today still teach this duality of God and the Devil, including Roman Catholicism, which is the religion I was raised in. My family was devoutly Catholic and this education from a young age placed God and the Devil at opposite polarities, each battling for my soul. If I didn't protect my heart through prayer, the Devil would bore into it and plant a dark seed there that would flourish over time. If I didn't attend church, I was going to hell. If I accepted the eucharist through another religion, I was ostracizing myself from the one true faith. If I had sex before marriage, I was a slut, a bad person, and a sinner. These were all messages I received as a child to strike fear in me.

As I studied religion in college through the concepts of war and feminism, I learned that these religions were historically used to conquer and control. Religion was used to assimilate the people of other nations into empires. It was used to keep various kings and other leaders in power. It was used to control women and children and elevate men through its patriarchal rules and structure. These were never the founding purposes of these religions, but rather the distortions of them over time.

I also discovered my own personal disdain and disinterest in a dual approach to a higher power. Over time I came to see that Roman Catholicism, as well as all or most of the Protestant faiths that were birthed from Catholicism, ultimately promote a belief that the Devil is as powerful as God. They believe that hell is as powerful as heaven, that sin is as powerful as prayer, and that darkness is as powerful as light.

But how could the Devil ever truly be as powerful as God, if God is truly all-powerful? The answer is that the Devil is an illusion. God is God, and the Devil is nothing, because God is love and the Devil is only separation from love.

The Devil and hell are merely distortions of God and heaven. They are arbitrary separations to explain an observable phenomenon, which is that sometimes bad things happen in the world, that sometimes we suffer, that sometimes karma is a bitch, that sometimes prayers are answered, and that all of this must be attributed to... something... right? Someone... right?

The truth of your higher power is that he is only love. Your higher power only offers heaven, only supports us in reuniting with him, and only desires to give us light.

We are going through another evolution of religion right now, to unity toward a higher power. The unity understanding of our higher power is the belief that our higher power is someone who loves us, supports us, and wants the best for us. He does not smite us when we "sin" (aka break some arbitrary rules that a small group of people created to keep much larger groups of people under control for generations). He does not send us goodness for being obedient nor does he send us suffering for stepping out of line.

Our higher power is not an abusive creator. He presents us with lessons and experiences that bring us closer to our desires and gives us infinite tries to pass the tests because he desires our collective success. He helps us transcend challenge and suffering and patiently asks us over and over again to choose his support and co-creation in our lives. He lovingly stays with us through our times of doubt and denouncement, much like a parent calmly sitting next to their child through a raging tantrum.

God loves us perfectly, supports us endlessly, and desires a deep and intimate relationship with us always.

This is not the God that many religions in their current form teach.

I recognize that these words may be very triggering to some people, which is not my intention. My goal is to show that the evolution of religion is to understand that the Devil is merely a separation we created in God. We gave God polarity because we needed someone to blame and shame when things went wrong for us. We distorted God in order to understand him more deeply.

But just as scientists are throwing out their current understanding of water, we too much throw out our current understanding of God through dual consciousness so we can evolve. That's what the ascension and twin soul journey is all about. We are recognizing that what we've been calling God and the Devil is actually just God, what we've been calling heaven and hell is actually just heaven, what we've been calling fear and love is actually just love. We needed those polarities to go deeper with these concepts, but through the Law of Polarity, we can now unify them and see them as the spectrums that they actually are.

INTEGRATING RELIGION AND SPIRITUALITY WITH THE LAW OF POLARITY

While it may seem like I'm down on religion, I'm not at all. Remember, Catholicism is what introduced me to the Twin Soul Trinity, something I will be eternally grateful for. Rather, I see that religion is evolving through spirituality. Spirituality, in many ways, is taking religion apart like a clock and looking at all its pieces, then reassembling them into a greater and evolved truth that matches the ascension of collective consciousness we are already experiencing as a planet.

Back in early 2018, I had the strange experience of attending two Catholic funerals about two weeks apart. I had not set foot in a Catholic church since basically the day of my wedding over eleven years earlier. During this absence of steady faith in my life, I had spent several years drifting between agnosticism and atheism, and several more years actively studying manifestation, tarot, astrology, twin souls, and telepathy. While at these two funerals, I got to experience Catholicism through a new lens and noticed a number of similarities to the spiritual work I had been doing.

I found this curious but didn't think much of it, until I went to Italy just a few weeks later. My entire life I had dreamed of going to the Vatican. Before 2018, if you had asked me what one place in the world I would travel to, the answer would have easily been the Vatican. It was a dream planted deep in my heart from a young age, as a young Catholic who wanted to understand the origins of the ideology that consumed her Sundays.

We happened to go to the Vatican on the day of my 34th birthday. I felt giddy with excitement as this was a dream come true for me. After spending most of the day touring the grounds, the museums, and St. Peter's Basilica, we found ourselves underground, in the Sacristy and Treasury Museum, surrounded by armed guards who would not allow us or anyone else to take pictures, flash or none.

Toward the end of the tour I noticed a large, heavy tome inside a glass-encased pedestal that had a familiar-looking cover. I stepped closer to it, aware of the guard standing nearby. It looked like The World card from the Rider-Waite tarot deck!

I would later learn that the image on the book was portraying Matthew, Mark, Luke, and John, writers of the Gospels, through their symbols of the angel, the eagle, the bull, and the lion, respectively. These four symbols can be found at the corners of The World card in most tarot decks that follow the Rider-Waite structure. This makes sense, of course, as tarot was originally a card game that became popular among wealthy families in Italy. These cards historically reflected Christian symbolism and only became associated with occult, and thus, frowned upon by the church, in the 18th century.

As I studied the cover of this book, everything clicked into place and I knew the message that my higher power was trying to send me. He had sent me to the two funerals and then all the way to the Vatican in Italy on my birthday, no less, because he wanted me to integrate my past and my present. He wanted me to see that he had tried to speak to me through Catholicism for so many years, with limited success. Then, when I shunned Catholicism, he found another way to speak to me, through tarot, astrology, manifestation, and more. He wanted me to understand that he was always there for me and always had been, walking next to me in life. He also wanted me to know that while religion and New Age spirituality seem to be dichotomous, they are truly just polarities on a spectrum. I was to have compassion for all the ways in which people communicate with him, as all are just tools. There is no separation, and I needed to unite my past and present within in order to move forward.

I am and will be forever appreciative of my background in Catholicism and the way it introduced me to my higher power, while at the same time understanding the religion's limitations and distortions. The Law of Polarity helped me understand that religion and spirituality are on a spectrum, thus they are the same. Both are simply the relationship we as a collective have with our higher power, who is also evolving just as we are. We have moved together from a multi-ality world (gods and goddesses) to a duality world (much of religion as we know it) to a unity world (the present and the future).

Many of us come to spirituality from a place of past trauma with religion. This is something that is likely to come up for healing before you unite with your twin soul. You cannot truly heal separation from your higher power if you are rejecting a large part of their history, evolution, and ascension.

If there are some triggering aspects of this section for you, take only what resonates for now. If you have a strong affiliation with a specific religion and are feeling friction, know that you are part of the evolution of your religion—your role and part to play in this evolution is being brought to your attention through this book. If you are feeling blame or shame around your religious upbringing or affiliation, have compassion for yourself. It is safe to learn, grow, and evolve.

THE TWIN SOUL TRINITY AND THE LAW OF POLARITY

Most twin soul literature describes the twin soul union as a divine partnership between two counterparts, one masculine and one feminine. These are not referring to male and female, but rather to masculine and feminine energies. These two polarities may seem dichotomous at first, but of course, they are actually on a spectrum. Just like hot and cold, the masculine partly defines the feminine and vice-versa. They are relative to each other. One cannot exist without the other, which means that the masculine cannot exist without the feminine, and vice-versa.

The Law of Polarity helps us understand that there is no difference between the masculine and feminine counterparts in the union. Not only are they the same and complimentary, but there is also no separation between them—that separation is an illusion.

The Law of Polarity describes the relationship between you and your twin soul. You are two polarities on a spectrum, meant to come as a pair, and meant to interact with the world relative to each other.

THE TWIN SOUL TRINITY

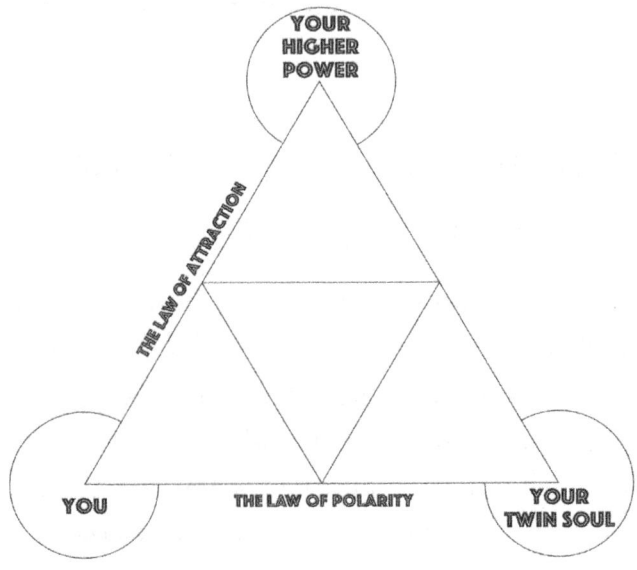

YOUR HIGHER POWER

THE LAW OF ATTRACTION

YOU   THE LAW OF POLARITY   YOUR TWIN SOUL

We will discuss the masculine and feminine counterparts in the twin soul union more deeply in the next chapter. If you accept for now that twin souls come to earth as a pair, masculine and feminine, then you can use the Law of Polarity to understand how they interact. For example, if you are the feminine counterpart, it would naturally follow that to attract your masculine counterpart, you need to choose your feminine polarity more deeply.

THE LAW OF CORRESPONDENCE

The Law of Correspondence is the meaning behind the phrase, "as above, so below." It states that your inner reality, which is truly just your relationship to your higher power (life, the Universe, God, Source, Spirit, your Creator), must be reflected in your outer reality. This is sometimes described as, "as within, so without."

The Law of Correspondence connects two relationships in the Twin Soul Trinity—the one between you and your higher power, and the one between you and your twin soul. It suggests that our relationship with our higher power, which exists "above," must also exist "below" on Earth. If we are romancing our higher power and being romanced by our higher power, then that romantic partnership must also exist on Earth as our twin soul.

THE TWIN SOUL TRINITY

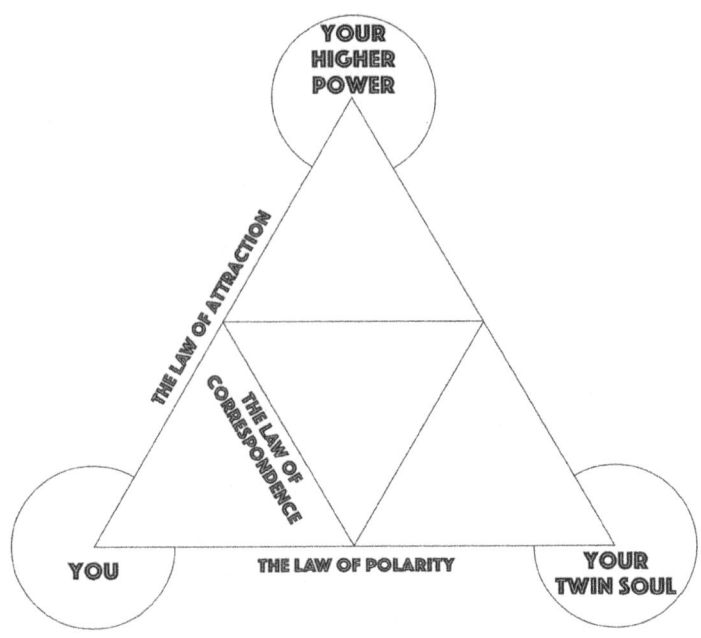

Let's expand this idea beyond twin souls to everything you desire. In truth, the Twin Soul Trinity does not place just your twin soul in the third point on the triangle. Every desire you have—wealth, purpose, your dream home, and more—can be placed at that third point because of the Law of Correspondence. In truth, the Twin Soul Trinity also describes your relationship between you, your higher power, and every aspect of your dream life, including your twin soul.

The Law of Attraction suggests that everything you truly desire is real and cannot be threatened, including your twin soul. The Law of Polarity suggests that separation doesn't exist between two polarities, such as you and your twin soul. And the Law of Correspondence suggests that your relationship with your higher power must exist in everything on Earth, including your twin soul. These three Universal Laws describe your personal experience with the Twin Soul Trinity, from your own vantage point. This is likely what you will or are experiencing in your physical reality on a daily basis, but it wouldn't be possible without the third relationship in the Twin Soul Trinity. In the next chapter, we'll go deeper into your twin soul's relationship to your higher power, and why it's so important to the Twin Soul Trinity.

JOURNALING PROMPTS

- What are your insights around the Law of Polarity and how it relates to the twin soul journey? How can you apply it to your understanding of who your twin soul is?

- What if you explored the polarity of love and fear?

  - Go all in on fear, ego, control for a day, choosing fear in everything you do. Express your disgust, complain loudly, and yell at people who make mistakes. Does it work and how does it feel?

- Go all in on love, peace, surrender for a day. Choose love in everything you do. Take care of yourself meticulously. Give to others wherever you can. Love every part of your body, home, work, play at the highest energy levels you can handle. Does it work and how does it feel?

- Do you agree that the Twin Soul Trinity can replace your twin soul with any true and permanent desire or dream of yours, and still conceptually work? Why or why not? Where do you desire clarity around this?

- What are your thoughts on the Law of Correspondence? Do you feel it unites the Law of Attraction and the Law of Polarity on the Twin Soul Trinity? Why or why not?

FEELING STUCK?

- **Learn more about the Twin Soul Trinity.** I've put together a page of resources that can take you deeper into these concepts, beyond the content of this book. Listen, watch, and read at http://cardreadingqueen.com/twin-soul-trinity/

Chapter Eight
HOW WE KNOW THE TWIN SOUL TRINITY EXISTS

We've gone deep into the Law of Attraction and the Law of Polarity, as well as connected the two using the Law of Correspondence to explain the connection between you and your higher power and you and your twin soul. In this chapter, I want to further connect the dots and explain the final pieces of the Twin Soul Trinity, including the relationship between your higher power and your twin soul as it relates to you.

As a reminder, everything in these chapters builds on what we already know from the Universal Laws that are popular in the New Age/New Thought movements. You can test each of these laws through the hundreds of books that have already been written about these 12 laws. Let's build on what we have so far and further explain the Twin Soul Trinity.

THE LAW OF GENDER

When I first came across the Law of Gender, I'll admit it—I was triggered. I like to think of myself as a progressive and accepting person, and I'm a big believer that gender is largely a construct that we are socialized into. I was bothered by and unsure of the masculine and feminine energies, even though I knew that masculine and feminine did not mean male and female and had nothing to do with your specific body, sexual organs, or sexual preferences. Why the duality, when twin souls is truly about union? Aren't the masculine and feminine energies just social constructs, and wouldn't those definitions ultimately merge if the two twin souls are one?

To be honest, I wasn't sure why twin souls had to come in specifically as a masculine and a feminine, but after reading about the Law of Gender, I found clarity. The Law of Gender says that the point of creation is a masculine energy and a feminine energy interacting. This can be at the spiritual, mental, emotional, or physical level. And the proof of this law is easily found in nature, where 99% of how things are created is with a pair of masculine and feminine counterparts.

If a famous artist from centuries ago painted a masculine and feminine into all of his paintings, we would come to understand this as his signature. If 500 years later, we found a painting that had no identification, but had the masculine and feminine painted in, and used the same signature style and strokes, we might be suspicious that the painting belonged to that same famous artist. We might use historical evidence such as other paintings, knowledge of the famous artist's whereabouts, or journal entries to attempt to trace and confirm the origin of the painting.

Similarly, we can use the history of consciousness, combining religious, philosophical, and scientific evidence to understand twin souls. Your higher power is not trying to trick you in the way things work. If you've heard of Occam's razor, then you may know that the simplest explanation is often the preferred one. Everything on earth is an expression of your higher power's preferences. The bible itself says that, "God made mankind in his own image, in the image of God he created them; male and female he created them (Genesis 1:27)." Your higher power desires to express itself in a certain way, and that way is largely through the two energies of the masculine and feminine.

There are exceptions of course, and there are exceptions around twin souls too. Not every twin soul partnership is between a single masculine and a single feminine. There can be more than two twin souls in a partnership, or there could be two feminines, two masculines, and so on.

But the Law of Gender says that the default, which applies to almost all twin soul partnerships, is one masculine and one feminine. Most likely, your twin soul partnership is one masculine and one feminine, and you are one of the two. This is simply the way your higher power likes to express themself in their creations. It is easiest for now, and until something deeper is revealed to you, to assume your twin soul partnership is between you and one other soul— your perfect divine counterpart.

THE TWIN SOUL TRINITY

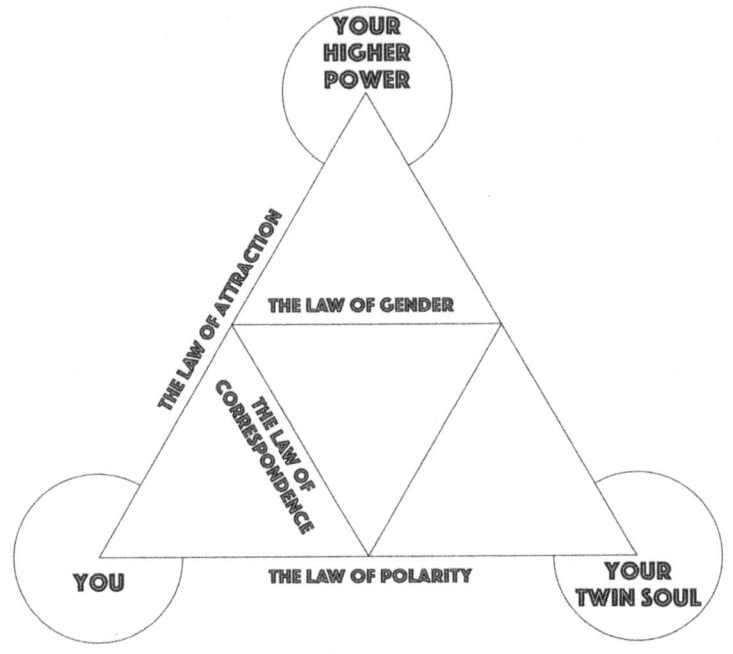

In the Twin Soul Trinity, The Law of Gender describes the relationship your higher power has with you and your twin soul. Your higher power created the two of you as a pair. Because of that, your higher power intended for the two of you to be together, united on Earth. Your higher power doesn't waste energy or create haphazardly, so you can be sure that you and your divine counterpart are meant to be together.

The thing that ultimately convinced me that twin souls came in pairs of masculine and feminine was the concept of the point of creation. In nature, the point of creation is deeply important. While virginal birth is possible and there are a handful of known cases of it in mammals held in captivity, it is not the preferred method of creation for your higher power. Science has shown us the purpose for this, which is that a creation—a human child, for example—is stronger and healthier when its DNA comes from two sources, a masculine and feminine, rather than one. You cannot create a human child without the two portions of DNA from two parents. Likewise, you cannot create anything in the world without the two energies of the masculine and feminine, ideally in balance.

Twin soul literature claims that you are always interacting with your twin soul, at least at the energetic level if not in the physical. The proof of that is right there in your life. If you are creating in your life—and remember, creating can include transformation, evolution, creation, destruction, and more—then there must be a partner in that creation. That partner is your twin soul, and you are energetically interacting with them at all times. As I write this book, for example, I'm not writing it by myself. I'm creating this book with my twin soul, regardless of whether he is physically present with me as I type. Our energies are interacting and I'm channeling this book through both of us. This is the truth of twin souls—we are one and there is no separation.

While the masculine and feminine are divine counterparts, they are also just labels to describe an experience. You don't necessarily need to know whether you are the masculine or the feminine; it is only useful to you in being able to better identify your counterpart, who would be the opposite of you. Furthermore, masculine and feminine has nothing to do with gender. For some time, I thought I was the masculine in my relationship because I had studied physics and computer science and I tended to be a more logical thinker. Over time, I've really come to understand that I'm the feminine in my relationship. If you are interested to discover whether you are the masculine or feminine in your relationship, you may be interested in my book, *Masculine vs. Feminine: Understanding the Masculine and Feminine Counterparts and How They Come Into Union in the Twin Soul Relationship (Twin Soul Hearts in Union #4).*

Because both you and your twin soul can access both the masculine and feminine energies of your relationship within, the more important concept when it comes to masculine and feminine is distorted versus divine. Globally, we largely still live under a patriarchy which places the masculine energy over the feminine energy. This has created both distorted masculine and distorted feminine patterns that we as a collective are trying to ascend. For example, many masculines believe that the best way to protect themselves is to cast the finger of blame; likewise, many feminines believe they can receive their good through seduction. These are two sides of the same distorted pattern.

Much of what you don't like or think is "toxic" about your divine counterpart has nothing to do with the masculine or the feminine, but rather a distorted masculine or distorted feminine pattern. Toxicity is not a person, it's a pattern. If you see toxicity in your counterpart, then you likely hold the other half of that distorted pattern within. This is good news, because it means you can heal it within you and you will eradicate the pattern in your relationship as a result. I have personally seen and done this multiple times in my own twin soul relationship. If you'd like to learn more about this, I walk you through 15+ distorted masculine and feminine patterns, as well as how to heal them, in my book, *Masculine vs. Feminine: Understanding the Masculine and Feminine Counterparts and How They Come Into Union in the Twin Soul Relationship (Twin Soul Hearts in Union #4)*. I also offer a Masculine-Feminine Balancing healing modality certification if you are a coach, healer, reader, or astrologer and want to learn a new healing modality that you can incorporate into your personal practices or use to serve your clients.

THE LAW OF DIVINE ONENESS

The Law of Divine Oneness states that we are all connected and that the way in which we interact with the world is rippled out beyond our immediate physical environment. In other words, we can affect everyone around us in a positive way if we ourselves are interacting positively, and affect everyone around us in a negative way if we ourselves are interacting negatively.

If you have any sort of interaction with your twin soul—and remember, at the least you are interacting with them energetically and spiritually at all times—then you are influencing and affecting them. This is true for anything and anyone you come into contact with, but it is especially true for your twin soul due to the deep connection that the two of you share. You have the ability to connect deeply and endlessly on all levels, which means the mirror is strong.

That means that whatever you are currently experiencing and whatever your current vibration is, your twin soul can only expand that as the two of you come together. If you are interacting negatively with your world, then uniting with your twin soul can only expand your negativity. If you are interacting positively with your world, then uniting with your twin soul can only expand your positivity.

This is why you may not be physically united with your twin soul right now. Check in with your vibration—would it truly be compassionate to you, them, or anyone else to expand your vibration as it is? If the answer is yes, then your higher power is supporting you in uniting physically because your higher power wants to expand and create with positivity. If the answer is no, then your higher power is supporting you in uniting physically by giving you situations, experiences, and messages that help you heal your wounding so you can interact positively, so it makes sense and is compassionate for you to unite with your twin soul.

When you physically unite with your twin soul, you will be affecting each other on all levels. This will lead both of you to rapid expansion. If the Twin Soul Trinity did not exist, this would cause chaos for your relationship, as rapid expansion and creation would take the two of you in different directions. But because you are twin souls, you choose the same every time. This means that as you change and affect the world around you, your twin soul changes and affects the world around them in the same exact way. This is the only way that twin souls would make sense. You have to make the same core choice, or else your paths would diverge as quickly as they crossed.

What this law is ultimately saying is that you can change your twin soul's relationship with your higher power just by changing yourself. Your twin soul's relationship with your higher power is the same as their relationship with life or with the Universe. If when you make a core choice, they also have to make the same core choice, then your choice is extremely powerful in changing their life, as well as yours.

THE TWIN SOUL TRINITY

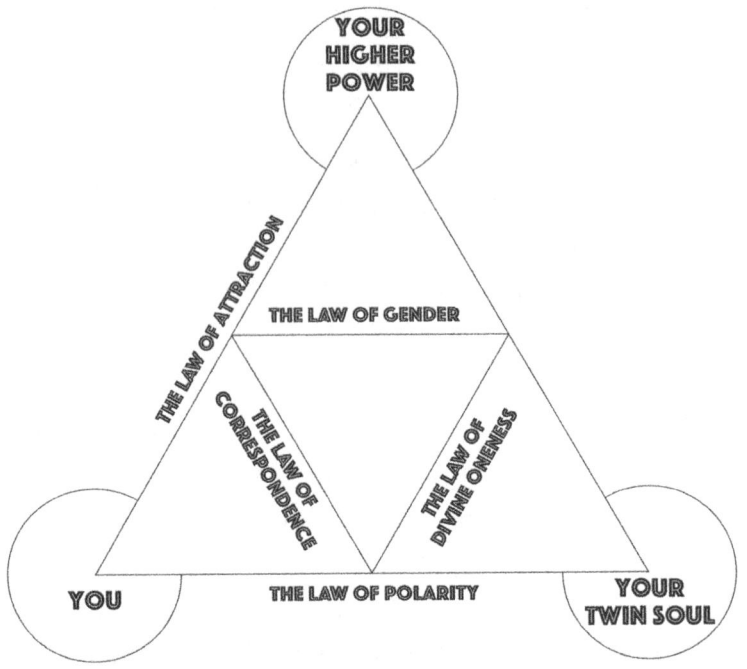

DIVINE ORDER

Throughout this book I've hinted at and implied the concept of divine order, but we haven't dived deep into it. Divine order is the belief that everything has its place, every person has their role, all is in alignment with no conflicts, and everything and everyone you truly desire in your heart is meant to be with you permanently.

There is no proof that divine order exists, but if

you believe in any sort of heaven, you have to believe in divine order. If there was no divine order in heaven, then two people could claim the same twin soul. This immediately creates control, competition, and scarcity, all of which are rooted in fear and not of God or heaven. This quickly spirals out of control if it becomes widespread, or if it were to describe the way heaven worked. Some people would get picked or claimed as a twin soul, but some wouldn't. Some people would get rejected by the person they think is their twin soul if there was more than one claim to a person. The person who had multiple people claiming them as their twin soul would have to rank their suitors, which creates hierarchy, which is also rooted in fear. This would end with a lot of unmatched individuals, which means a lot of souls would not receive or be perfectly loved. All of sudden, heaven is starting to sound a lot like Earth!

Earth as it is currently seems very chaotic and random. This is an illusion of course, as heaven on Earth is possible, if we decide as a collective to put everything back in its divine order. Chaos and randomness are distorted order, born out of ego and control. On earth, there are people who claim more or less wealth than they divinely need, people who overeat, undereat, or otherwise abuse their bodies, people who compete with others for love, attention, or pleasure, people who overindulge and chase false highs, and so much more. Earth currently exists in distorted order rather than divine order, with humanity trying to create order largely through fear and control.

That's what the ascension process hopes to change. When spiritual people talk about New Earth, what they are really describing is bringing the divine order of heaven to earth. This means that there are specific things that are meant for you—your twin soul, your divine purpose, your dream home, your perfect expression of beauty, your divine bank account balance, and more—and your ascension is truly just getting your personal life in divine order. Divine order on the personal level is becoming the perfect expression of the truth of who you are, here on earth.

Heaven cannot exist without divine order, and you cannot experience heaven now without believing in divine order. To not believe in divine order is to believe in distorted order, which is just randomness, coincidence, chaos, lack of power, lack of control, and victimhood. I have experienced both in my life, and because of that I will always choose to believe in heaven and divine order. Your twin soul is one beautiful piece of that divine order that your heart truly longs to experience.

DIVINE ORDER AND FREE WILL

How can you be both a co-creator in your life (aka have "free will") and also believe in divine order, which basically states that you have specific things that are meant for you? How can you both follow your higher power's plan for you and experience life, excitement, and choice on earth?

Some people see divine order as a cage, but for me, believing in divine order gives me the greatest freedom and security in life. Divine order is actually the map that tells me the exact path I can take to receive the peace and happiness that I desire in life. I don't want to veer away from my greatest peace and happiness—that is illogical. If presented with my favorite flavor of ice cream, and a random flavor of ice cream, why wouldn't I choose my favorite flavor every time?

An experiment by Columbia professor and choice expert Sheena Iyengar demonstrated that more patrons were willing to stop by a jam booth displaying 24 flavors, but those who stopped by the booth only displaying 6 flavors were six times more likely to buy some jam. Having choice may attract us, much like a temporary or false high. It ultimately doesn't move us forward or make us happier in life.

To me, the real enjoyment of life is in going deep with one choice in each category—your twin soul, your divine body and health, your dream home, your divine purpose, your ideal wealth level, and so on. My twin soul is endlessly fascinating to me, as is my divine purpose, as is my divine home, and so on. I deeply desire to receive all of my love and abundance in *this* lifetime. I want to experience joy and peace *now*. I do not want to waste time and energy learning through attracting experiences mired in needless suffering and contrast. No thanks!

Perhaps you feel differently, and that's okay. My observation of myself is that when I thought I desired variety in any of these areas of my life, I was really acting from a place of wounding and scattering my energy. I noticed this when I was flirtier in my late teens and early twenties, scattering my attention to random people. I also noticed this when I job-hopped from position to position, never really establishing myself or my expertise at any one company. This made sense for me as a young adult, because I was learning and finding my way, but ultimately, it left me very empty and numbed out. I was healing through contrast because I didn't know I could just heal within. The minute I committed to my true divine purpose and my true twin soul, my life got so much richer and juicier. There are always new and interesting things to experience and explore in my writing career, and the same is true with my twin soul. I find peace and security in knowing that my good and abundance can never leave me.

THE LAST PIECE OF THE TWIN SOUL TRINITY

In writing this book, I asked myself what the relationship between your higher power and your twin soul, represented with a single line in the Twin Soul Trinity, truly represented from the perspective of You. At first, I considered whether that relationship was simply the Law of Attraction again, and found that it was but only from the perspective of your twin soul. From your perspective, it could not be the Law of Attraction, because you can't manifest for someone else.

So what do you really want in your twin soul's relationship with your higher power? You want:

- Someone who is your dream partner who matches every desire in your heart (Law of Attraction)

- Someone who can meet you on every level (Law of Polarity)

- Someone who expands in love as you love life and your higher power, who helps you create your heaven on earth (Law of Correspondence)

- Someone who is a real person who matches you energetically and helps you create in the physical (Law of Gender)

- Someone who grows in the same direction as you at all times (Law of Divine Oneness)

In other words, you want someone who makes the same energetic or core choice as you. Someone who is yours by divine order, who no one else can claim. But there is no Universal Law for that...

THE LAW OF ALIGNMENT

I believe that the last piece of the Twin Soul Trinity rests on coming into alignment with the divine order of things. The Law of Alignment is a very new thought and not something I've read about in other books. At the same time, this law is built on the foundations of New Age and New Thought, which I've demonstrated over the last several chapters.

THE TWIN SOUL TRINITY

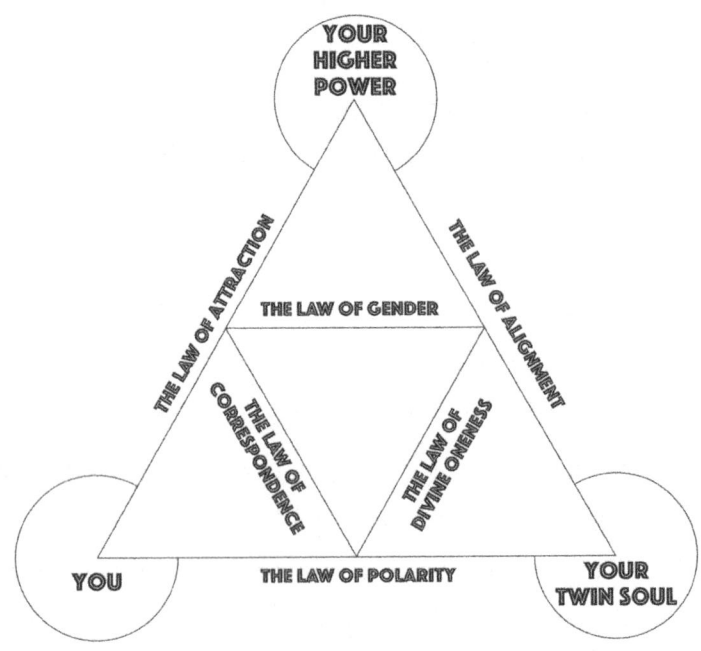

The Law of Alignment is the understanding that as you grow closer to your higher power, everything that's already yours by design (and by true desire)— all of which you are merely healing separation from— must come into your reality. This includes your twin soul, but also includes many other aspects of your divine design.

The Law of Alignment also says that as you heal and reveal your true self and the illusion of separation from your higher power, your life can only get better and more perfect for you. This is because you continue to align to your divine design, which is the blueprint of your ultimate happiness.

THE EVOLUTION OF NEW THOUGHT/NEW AGE

Wait a second... did she just write a new Universal Law?! No, not really—I'm honestly not that clever. What I've done instead is named something that's easily observable when you take the other 5 Universal Laws into consideration and blend them with the concept of divine order, which is also embedded in New Age and New Thought.

I believe that there is an evolution of the New Thought/New Age movements that is happening right now. This makes sense, as your higher power is always evolving and so are we, both personally and collectively as a planet. Many people believe and see evidence that the planet is ascending at a faster rate than ever before, and science and technology supports this evolution.

The evolution of the New Thought/New Age movements centers around divine order, and more specifically, moving everything around us from chaos or distorted order to divine order.

In revisiting each of the five Universal Laws we've discussed, and where New Thought/New Age seems to get it wrong or distort it, I see:

LAW OF ATTRACTION

For the Law of Attraction, you can't attract and permanently hold anything or anyone you want. There is little point in attracting something that you cannot hold, because in your heart all that you really want to attract is your higher power manifested as abundance and love here on earth. Attracting something you can't permanently hold is just a false or temporary high, which can only make you feel good for a time. It is largely a waste of energy to chase these false highs. You can only attract and permanently hold what is yours by design, so you must uncover yourself to know where to invest your energy.

LAW OF POLARITY

We used to collectively believe in both God and the Devil, as purported by religion, but we are shifting from duality consciousness to unity consciousness, which is a shift from polarity to spectrums. The Devil does not and cannot exist because that would mean that God is not all-powerful. The Devil was always merely a representation of how close or far you were from God, but there was only ever one God. Likewise, everything that looks like it has polarity is actually the same, which is incredibly relieving!

LAW OF CORRESPONDENCE

Heaven and Earth used to be considered very separate spaces. Religion put gates on heaven, while spirituality relinquished heaven to the 5th dimension. As part of ascension, however, the above is actually merging with the below. That's why more twin souls are uniting on Earth now, because we are beginning to understand that a good life with a soulmate partner is not as satisfying as a divinely ordered life with your perfect divine partner. As a collective, we have ascended striving in favor of thriving, which is what enables so many of us to make the next leap in consciousness to understanding divine order.

LAW OF GENDER

While most of creation starts with the masculine and feminine, there are exceptions that are also perfect. Furthermore, the physical body is an illusion, which means that male is not masculine and female is not feminine. We are learning to recognize the energies over the illusion of flesh through LGBTQIA+ relationships. We are also learning that we cannot pair off people through control, and that uniting with your twin soul is a process that puts your higher power first rather than putting societal expectations or institutions first.

LAW OF DIVINE ONENESS

Your higher power is in everything and everyone. You are also one with everything and everyone else. But there are degrees of oneness because of divine order and its necessary existence in heaven. You are most one with your twin soul, due to the nature and promise of what heaven is. Divine order explains why your twin soul is truly your perfect mirror.

DIVINE ORDER: THE KEY TO THE LAW OF ALIGNMENT

Divine Order is the critical missing piece to each of these laws and how they are evolving. The Law of Alignment, not currently covered explicitly in New Age/New Thought, is really only saying that divine order exists and that as you grow your relationship to your higher power, your reality must move from chaos or distorted order to divine order. This creates your truest happiness the same way cleaning your home would. By choosing divine order, you are also choosing peace, love, joy, and freed energy.

TEST THE TWIN SOUL TRINITY

You don't have to take my word for it when it comes to the Twin Soul Trinity. While I consider the Twin Soul Trinity a foundational piece of the twin soul journey, you can explore it on your own to see if it resonates.

Here are some ideas of how you can test the Twin Soul Trinity in your own life:

- **Look at your upsets -** Whenever you're upset with your twin soul, you can see if there's a thread around the same upset with your higher power as well. Notice where the upset applies to both... Then test whether working on one relationship brings peace to the other, and vice-versa.

- **Go all in with your higher power for a few months -** Do your healing work and build your relationship with them. See who comes toward you and who moves away in the physical. Observe with no attachment. Your twin soul will move toward you as you heal, as will your soul family and others in the twin soul vibration, even if they are not permanent relationships. Everyone else will move away.

- **Keep trying to get your twin soul without your higher power -** If it's working for you and makes you happy, keep going for your twin soul and trying to create in the physical, without your higher power's help. If you are able to achieve peace and happiness this way, perhaps the Twin Soul Trinity isn't real! If this isn't working for you, why not try another way that assumes the Twin Soul Trinity is real?

JOURNALING PROMPTS

- Do you believe the Twin Soul Trinity exists? Why or why not? What would improve your clarity around how twin souls really work?

- What are your thoughts on the Law of Gender and how it relates to twin souls?

- What are your thoughts on the Law of Divine Oneness and how it relates to twin souls?

- How does the concept of Divine Order feel to you? Is it liberating, claustrophobic, or something else? How do you believe heaven works?

- What do you think of the Law of Alignment to describe the last piece of the Twin Soul Trinity? Do you believe that as you grow toward your higher power, you must attract everything you truly desire, from your twin soul to your divine purpose to your perfect wealth, to you? If not, what do you believe instead?

FEELING STUCK?

- **Learn more about the Twin Soul Trinity.** I've put together a page of resources that can take you deeper into these concepts, beyond the content of this book. I review the last several chapters in my 4-part series, Are Twin Flames Real?! Listen, watch, and read at http://cardreadingqueen.com/twin-soul-trinity/

- **Dive deeper into the Masculine and Feminine aspects of the journey.** My book on this topic is called *Masculine vs. Feminine: Understanding the Masculine and Feminine Counterparts and How They Come Into Union in the Twin Soul Relationship (Twin Soul Hearts in Union #4).* This series dives deep into 15+ distorted patterns in the masculine and feminine dynamic, specifically as it relates to twin souls. Check out the *Twin Soul Hearts in Union* series here: http://cardreadingqueen.com/books/

- **Check out my healing modality certifications.** I offer four healing modalities that you can find more information on at http://cardreadingqueen.com/certifications/. The healing modality certifications I offer are:

- Core Wound Healing

- Masculine-Feminine Balancing

- Tarot: Concentration in Love, Romance, and Relationships

- Astrology: Concentration in Love, Romance, and Relationships

Chapter Nine

THE OBSTACLES BLOCKING YOUR TWIN SOUL UNION

When I was 20 years old, I broke up with an ex-boyfriend who I thought was the love of my life. At the time, I didn't understand why things kept falling apart between us when we seemed to love each other and want a future together. The pain had become too great, however, and I saw no choice but to leave the relationship to end the pain.

The breakup did end the pain, temporarily. But over the years, I thought about this ex a lot. I spent several years blaming him for not choosing me. Then, my blame turned to myself and all the mistakes I made in the relationship to drive us apart. I spent a lot of time in, "if I had only..."

Finally, I came around to blaming my higher power, God, for the relationship. At this point, I could not see how the ex had ever loved me to begin with. If he had truly loved me the way I loved him, wouldn't he have come back at some point? Hadn't I trusted God to bring us back together when the timing was better, or when the ex finally figured out that I had worth to him and he couldn't live without me?

I believed that God had brought this relationship into my life just to cause me suffering and shatter my heart, over and over again. I regretted every moment of the relationship and begged God to send me back in time so I could undo the relationship by never entering it in the first place. I believed I could never heal all the pain this relationship caused me, and I believed that I would never truly get over my ex, no matter how many times I moved on or dated other people or cut cords or wrote letters and burned them or thought of the lyrics to "Twinkle Twinkle Little Star" when he popped into my mind.

Through this experience I found, as many people do, that the absence of pain is not the presence of peace. I had never truly dealt with the breakup. I had pushed the pain so far down into my subconscious that I was numb to it, but that didn't mean that I had peace in its place.

And this makes sense, because most techniques society teaches to get over someone are rooted in numbing out to the pain. We are told to block, go no contact, stop checking social media, distract ourselves, hook up with other people, cut them out of our lives, and more. In other words, we are told to numb out, numb out, ignore the pain, avoid, numb out, numb out, escape, distract.

But numbing out doesn't work long-term. It only buries the pain in your subconscious, where that pain then drives you and what you attract into your reality.

I numbed out to this particular breakup and it truly got me nowhere. It was needless suffering, endless tears, and a buildup of negative emotions and shame. It drove me to struggle with vulnerability and accepting love in all my later relationships. It made me feel worthless and unworthy of anything, from love, to money, to health, to purpose.

When I finally accepted responsibility for what had happened, without blaming and shaming myself or anyone else, the situation finally changed. I made the true choice to heal *all* of my feelings around the situation at the core and I found that *all* of my bad feelings were inside me, there long before the relationship even happened.

I realized I was completely and totally projecting my pain onto this person and always had been. I reflected back to my actions during our relationship and saw that I was trying to get everything I needed from this person and blaming them, when I couldn't give what I needed to myself. I realized there was truly no amount of love and attention they could have given me that could satiate my desire, because I couldn't give that love and attention to myself.

I was trying to make this person my source, when

only my higher power could be my source. And every way in which this ex hurt me—and I had a long list—was the projection of his pain and wounding onto me.

When I really began to understand this at the core of my being, I finally saw that this ex had loved me to the best of his ability for the entirety of our relationship. There were areas in which I couldn't truly receive his love, because I didn't love myself in those places. There were areas where he couldn't receive my love because he didn't love himself there.

This understanding ultimately gave me peace with this relationship. The peace extended to compassion for myself and how I had hurt this person, forgiveness for him and how he had hurt me, and restored trust and faith in my higher power who had brought us together and then allowed us to part.

No matter how long you have been on the twin soul journey, you've probably experienced intense pain and possibly even one or a few dark nights of the soul. When you begin to actively heal and this pain comes to the surface, it can feel really bad and overwhelming. I encourage you, however, to persist in your healing work. Many believe that this work makes you feel bad, but the healing work is actually the medicine; it makes you feel better. The wounding is the source of the pain. The healing is the source of the releasing of that pain. The healing is where you will find true and permanent peace, so that your past pain and trauma can no longer control you.

WHERE DO WOUNDS COME FROM?

All of what upsets us and disturbs our inner peace can be traced back to a separation from our creator.

On the non-spiritual level, this could be our parents, as they created us and brought us into the world. Many people do inner child wounding work to heal patterns they've co-created and internalized with their parents.

The "parents as creators" path also extends into others. In childhood, these are authority figures in our lives and can include parents, grandparents, aunts and uncles, older siblings, and teachers and other mentors. It can also include peers, classmates, close friends, and younger siblings.

As we graduate from childhood, the people closest to us will affect us the most. This can include our spouses, exes, bosses, coworkers, friends, acquaintances, and more.

On a spiritual level, this could be our higher source of power, such as God, the Universe, Source, Spirit, our Creator, our higher self or soul, or whatever or whomever we worship. Again, we can co-create our experiences with our creators, and those creators can manifest in the physical for us through any relationship or situation here on earth.

In both definitions of creator, the reality is that we are the co-creators of our lives and experiences. Healing comes from both forgiving our creator and forgiving ourselves. As we make these relationships right, we change the patterns we have fallen into and we heal our separation from our creator(s). This creates healing overall, backward and forward in time, and we are able to move through our lives in greater peace and balance.

The further back we go to the point of creation of our wounding, ideally our higher power or creator, the more we are able to heal. It's the difference between breaking off a twig of a tree versus cutting down an entire branch. When you go back to the creator level, you can actually uproot the wounding or trauma completely. I share more about the specific process of healing in the next chapter.

HEALING THROUGH INNER WORK VS. HEALING THROUGH OUTER WORK

There are two basic ways to heal or grow as a person: the inner work versus the outer work.

Healing through the outer work is attracting situations that can provide lessons for growth. For example, instead of doing inner work to discover what you truly want in a relationship, you may instead just date a lot of people and learn what you don't want through those experiences. Doing the outer work, sometimes called healing through contrast, is the way that most humans heal and grow. This is especially true for anyone not or not yet on an active ascension or twin soul journey.

Healing through the inner work is going within to actively heal your wounding through finding and uprooting false beliefs and self-sabotage. This is the preferred method of most spiritual people and those on the twin soul or ascension journey, because it usually brings peace and love to you significantly faster than the outer work. For example, if you want to know where you should live next, it's much easier to do the inner work on that question than it is to move to each of the places you're considering to test them out.

In truth, the inner work is not better or worse than the outer work. It's your choice to make and either choice can work in any situation. My preference is to try to heal through the inner work first, using the tools I describe in the next two chapters. If I'm feeling stuck on doing the inner work, I will choose contrast or the outer work to help move the energy forward.

Your healing is going to find you eventually, so never worry about taking the wrong path. You truly can't. Your journey is always going to unfold perfectly for you.

FALSE BELIEFS PEOPLE HAVE ABOUT DOING THE INNER WORK AND THE OUTER WORK

Healing through one of these pathways is a critical part of the twin soul journey. If you study the next several chapters on healing, you will have the physical manifestation of your twin soul union quickly. But there are a lot of ways people get frustrated with the healing process, which causes them to quit the twin soul journey. Most of this is rooted in false beliefs, so I want to quickly address those before getting into the healing part.

#1 - HEALING IS A WAY TO BLAME AND SHAME YOURSELF

I've found blame and shame around wounding to be an insidious false belief in both myself and others. Blame and shame have no place in healing, and if you are blaming and shaming yourself for your wounding, you are likely doing the same to others and especially to your twin soul. This is never going to attract your twin soul to you, nor is it going to bring you peace or love. So let's break it down!

First, there is no blame at the spiritual level because you are in full control of your reality at the spiritual level. You'll likely feel resistance to this and I've heard everything from, "I can't change my twin soul's behavior," to "but I don't want my twin soul to be dating someone else!" to "but what about starving children in Africa?!"

In all of these questions there is a thread of blame—do you see it? It doesn't matter what your resistance to my statement is, because it always comes back to two options: either something in your life that you don't like is your twin's fault, or something in your life that you don't like is your higher power's or God's fault.

We deeply fear taking responsibility for our reality as it is, because if we truly took full responsibility for our reality we would have to see the shadow sides of ourselves and do the inner or outer work to heal it.

Next, there is no shame at the spiritual level because your full expression of yourself is welcome and loved at the spiritual level. The third person we love to blame for our problems is—you guessed it—ourselves! This is the completion of the Twin Soul Trinity. This also does not attract your twin soul to you, because you are your twin soul.

If you are shaming yourself, you likely struggle with the idea that you are making mistakes, growing, and healing by design. You are truly a child of your higher power and an innocent. You are meant to make mistakes; it's natural, normal, and what you came to this planet to do.

Another way I see people blame and shame themselves is by beating themselves up for past mistakes, having regret about the past, wishing they had chosen differently and wondering if it would have made a difference in the outcome, questioning their ascension path and higher power, and more. All of these are just the same blame and shame but for contrast or outer work. You are specifically believing (falsely) that doing the inner work would have been a better option, a faster option, or would have saved you pain or grief. You can't possibly know that this is true, which is why it's best to assume that your path is perfect for you, no matter how windy or broken it seems as you are traveling it.

#2 - HEALING IS A WAY TO PUT UP WITH ALL YOUR TWIN'S SHIT LIKE A DOORMAT

Many people on this journey talk about the need for boundaries from their toxic twin soul as a means of self-love. They tend to set boundaries from a place of control, either trying to change their twin soul's behavior (which is truly just an ultimatum) or trying to quell or numb out to their own feelings about the behavior. The problem with this is that boundaries must be set from a place of love and peace. Setting boundaries any other way will result in your twin soul continuing to act out in the exact way that you dislike. I go into more detail about this in Chapter 12, which is all about boundaries with yourself and others.

So then what actually works? How do you get your twin soul to stop acting or treating you a certain way? The only answer is healing, as healing is the path to loving yourself and setting boundaries that actually work. If you are truly choosing to love yourself, then your true twin soul has no choice but to do the same. This is incredibly empowering, as it means that you never have to experience toxicity from your permanent lover.

We deeply fear loving ourselves in this way as the more we love ourselves, the more we reveal the truth of all our connections, including those with a twin soul, to ourselves. If you are setting ultimatums (a boundary from a place of fear), you are saying, "if you do or don't do X, I will respond with Y." It's a threat and a condition to your love. If you are setting boundaries from a place of love, however, you are saying, "You can do or don't do X, and I will love you anyway through a healthy boundary, and I will heal myself to rid us of this thread, and I will never give up on us, because we are true twin souls." With the latter, the energy is different because:

- You truly believe that your twin soul is your perfect mirror and showing you yourself through their actions

- You are committed to healing and doing your work because you believe that your true twin soul will then mirror back the love you give yourself

- You unconditionally love your twin soul and know that you are in it together with them, permanently

When you realize this, you see that your twin is acting the way they are in your reality only because you have a matching pattern. No one else can create in your reality, and no one else can change the dynamic between you and your twin soul but you. As you heal, the person you think is your twin soul will either step up as your true twin or vibrate away as a false twin. This is challenging because we often have deep attachments to our false twins!

#3 - HEALING IS PAINFUL AND REQUIRES SUFFERING

Healing may feel painful, but healing is the only true way to release the pain that you already feel within yourself. This pain comes from wounding, false beliefs, and self-sabotage. And in order to heal it, you do have to reveal it and feel it—this is the part that many do not like.

Why is healing the only way though? Can't you just suppress or repress the pain and wounding? And doesn't that feel good as well, in many ways?

Many people do find relief from the pain by pushing their wounding to the subconscious. Unfortunately, this is numbing to your feelings and at best, a temporary relief. The only way to feel permanent relief from your pain is to release it, rather than to bury it inside you. Your body is not a good container for your emotions, and to use and abuse your body this way is to create physical disease within your body.

This pain will also drive your reality from your subconscious. It gives you the illusion of control, but truly, the pain is what's in control, not you.

We deeply fear driving our reality from a place of consciousness versus a place of subconsciousness because we fear how powerful we are to transform our realities.

When confronting this journey, if you have fear around what pain you might uncover, consider that the pain is already there in a set amount. It doesn't matter how you heal it as healing it is only about re-vealing it, feeling it, and releasing it. You can move through the pain in any way you wish; time is an il-lusion and your pain comes up for healing in a divine order. There is no schedule to keep up with and no authority to judge your progress. Every effort you make to heal lessens the pile of wounding and pain, so you are always better off from doing a healing exercise. Healing cannot hurt you; it can only help you feel better permanently. And every effort to heal, no matter the means and no matter the size, gives you another piece of your permanent and everlasting peace.

#4 - IF YOU OR YOUR TWIN HEAL THROUGH CONTRAST, YOU'LL SLOW DOWN YOUR JOURNEY

I've seen a number of twins, particularly femi-nines, who really want their masculine to do their inner healing work rather than healing through con-trast. But part of unconditional love is allowing your twin to choose to heal through the means they need to, including through contrast.

The biggest examples of this are things like break-ing up with you, cheating on you, getting married to someone else, and/or having children with someone else. And while I don't deny that these are incredi-bly painful experiences, it's important to know that you can always find a way to be with your twin, no matter your physical situation. Healing through contrast cannot take you down the wrong path. It is not "harder" to undo or work through as there is no hierarchy of wounding; no wound is truly "harder" to heal than another. Your path is always perfect for you and you can't mess up things with your twin or with any of your heart's desires.

Furthermore, part of this journey is believing and understanding that your higher power wants you to unite with your twin soul. Your higher power is supportive in you moving toward your twin soul and all of your desires. No choice aside from death is truly permanent as you are the co-creator of your reality, and even with death, it is only the choice to end this lifetime; you can be born again and continue to do this work in the next life.

Another version of this false belief is that it'll take longer for your twin soul to heal through contrast, so it's wasting time or it's happening in divine timing. But you don't know if inner work or contrast is the fastest way to heal through an upset—sometimes contrast does move you or your twin soul forward faster than sitting in a room and spinning on your healing!

Healing does not occur in divine timing, at least not in the sense that you have to wait for your twin soul to come around. It occurs in divine order, and you can take as much time as you want with each wound as time is ultimately an illusion. You can control the pace of your journey by not taking your upsets so seriously and by working through them as they come up. This is true no matter how big your upset is. Heal it now; the additional layers will come up in divine order. Then, heal those. Don't make a big fuss or drama about it, as having upsets is a natural part of being a human, just as refilling the gas tank is a natural part of driving a car.

The next chapter takes you deeper into the healing process.

JOURNALING PROMPTS

- Have you done any core wound healing work before or studied the wounding tree? What did you learn from those experiences that match up with what I'm sharing in this chapter?

- Do you have resistance to the inner work versus the outer work? What is at the root of this resistance?

- What are your false beliefs around wounding and healing? Has anything in this chapter helped to shift those beliefs, or do you still have questions? How can you get clarity on your questions so you can truly understand and sink deeper into this work?

FEELING STUCK?

- **Get the Twin Soul Encouragement Deck.** It's not easy to do the healing work—I get it! I have been in resistance to healing work in the past, questioning whether it was easier to numb out instead of investing more deeply. This deck lovingly shares messages that will gently tune you to the twin soul vibration. You can pull cards virtually from all of my decks for free, or you can learn more about a physical copy of the deck at http://twinsouloracle.com

- **Check out the Core Wound Wheel Cheat Sheet** which helps you identify and name the wounding you are experiencing now. This can be extremely helpful in getting you to stop numbing out to potential separation consciousness that is holding you back from your union. Get the cheat sheet at http://cardreadingqueen.com/core-wound-wheel/

Chapter Ten

HOW TO HEAL AND LOVE YOURSELF

S o what exactly is the inner work, and how do you heal the things that trigger you? In my experience, there are lots of tools that will show you how to heal, but there's very little written to explain *why* the tools work.

Every tool I've seen for healing encapsulates some or all of what I'm about to share—my 5U Healing Process for healing all of your core wounding. The 5U Healing Process takes you through the five phases of healing: Upset, Uproot, Unmask, Union, Upheaval. This process will help you go from upset to healed quickly and completely, and you can adapt it to any modality that you prefer. This means that you can use this process with journaling, meditation, tarot or astrology, religion, energy healing, or anything else.

This process shows you how to move through

your upsets and use the other tools provided to explore what is currently subconscious to you. Remember, a wound is simply a subconscious pattern that is blocking you from becoming your true self.

I use this process with many modalities, but my primary modality is writing down my healing efforts using the Reflection Journaling Practice, which I cover in the next chapter. While I recommend writing out your healing when you are first beginning to use these tools, please know that you won't be writing it out forever, as eventually you will have far fewer upsets to heal and you will have enough experience with these tools to do the work in your head.

THE 5U HEALING PROCESS IS (IN OVERVIEW):

Below, I share the five phases of healing: Upset, Uproot, Unmask, Union, Upheaval. I also share the steps or bullets that are covered by the phase so you can adapt this process to any healing modality you choose. In the rest of this chapter, I take you deeper into each of the five phases so you truly understand the exact process of how to heal your wounding.

PHASE 1: UPSET

- Recognizing that you are in wounding, reacting from wounding, playing out a pattern of wounding

- Deciding that you'd like to heal it and feel peace, change the pattern

- Bringing the subconscious to the conscious and identifying the wound

- Naming the wound

- Identifying the emotions around the wound (a wound without emotions has no charge and is unlikely to be creating a pattern for you)

- Agreeing that the wounding is no longer serving you and you'd like to make a change

PHASE 2: UPROOT (RATIONAL 3D UNDOING)

- Identifying the beliefs you've formed because of the wound

- Assuming that you have identified false beliefs. Does it matter if it's the truth? No, because it no longer serves you

- Flipping the rock up on your beliefs and finding the falsity of the beliefs

- Unhooking yourself from the stories that you've told yourself due to the false belief

- Understanding how another's wounding may have helped co-create your experiences

- Uprooting and eradicating the false beliefs from your thought patterns. What other possibilities are there for the truth?

- Choosing the most positive story you can and staying open to the possibilities

PHASE 3: UNMASK (EMOTIONAL 5D UNDOING)

- Revealing the true source of the false belief(s) surrounding the wound (every false belief leads back to yourself or your creator(s))

- Entering the healing process around that pain sincerely through unmasking yourself as the source for your own pain

- Forgiving yourself and others for the false beliefs and wounds you've formed (or co-created with another)

PHASE 4: UNION

- Making a new and empowered choice by choosing a new belief that serves you

- Finding supporting evidence for that belief to create healing momentum

- Feeling forgiveness, compassion, and gratitude for the false beliefs

- Releasing them false beliefs with love

- Coming back into union with yourself, others, and humanity

- Committing to your new choice permanently by taking action aligned with the new choice every day

PHASE 5: UPHEAVAL

- Processing and integrating your healing into your daily life

- Reclaiming the parts of yourself you've lost due to this wound

- Re-triggering and reprocessing the onion layers of the wound

- Shifting your patterns and allowing people, situations, and experiences to vibrate out of your reality

- Mourning any challenging changes as you leave an old version of you behind

Studying the 5U Healing Process will make you an advanced student at healing your own core wounds, false beliefs, and upsets. You can use this deep understanding of healing work to create your own routines and practices that support the way you prefer to heal. You can also use this understanding to help others in your life heal their wounding and pain. And finally, you can use this advanced understanding to grow toward your twin soul—all you have to do is heal every upset as it comes up using the techniques I teach in the 5U Healing Process.

PHASE 1: UPSET

An upset is something you experience that triggers emotion in you—usually around shame, embarrassment, anger, hurt, worry, anxiety, fear. An upset can be current or something from the past that you still feel pain over. When you are first starting out with your active inner healing work, you may want to go back to things that happened in the past in your key relationships, especially if they caused you a great deal of pain. Finding relief from these past events can bring you a great deal of peace in the present, as you are cutting off the wound at the branch rather than breaking off twigs.

STEP 1: IDENTIFYING THE WOUND

To identify and put words to your wound, you must answer a few basic questions about the wound for yourself.

WHO ARE YOU ATTRIBUTING THE WOUND TO?

We are usually attributing, associating, or blaming our hurt and pain on someone or something else. There are five tiers of this, ranging from the most powerful to hurt us (our creator) down to the least powerful to hurt us (acquaintances and strangers we interact with in daily life).

- **Tier 1:** God, the universe, a higher power, yourself

- **Tier 2:** Parents, step-parents, adoptive parents and legal guardians

- **Tier 3:** Siblings, exes, best friends

- **Tier 4:** Grandparents, uncles/aunts, cousins, teachers, bosses, coworkers

- **Tier 5:** Whoever is immediately in front of you

Please note that this doesn't mean those in the lower tiers cannot cause extremely traumatic events in your life or deeply hurt your feelings—unfortunately they can!

What it does mean, however, is that if you experience something on Tier 5, there is always a path back through the tiers all the way to Tier 1. In other words, you've experienced this same trauma through someone else on each of the tiers.

If you can have an upset with someone on Tier 2, however, you only need to trace it back through one tier to Tier 1. You do not need to trace it forward, as once you heal at Tier 1, it will create a domino effect on all the other tiers. (A friend and I call this, cutting the wound off at the branch rather than breaking off the twigs causing the pain.)

You may also find yourself attributing pain to a situation that doesn't have a personified actor. This is common with illness, accidents, and systemic challenges. For these, you can look at Tier 1 toward your higher power, or look toward doctors, actors in the system, and so on for actors with whom you might be placing blame on.

Finally, you may be tracing the wound back to yourself. This is common if you find yourself still in healing around blame and shame. It is okay if this is where your upset lies, but I've also found that this can be a way to numb out and ultimately bypass your true feelings. If you have a tendency to turn the finger on yourself, I encourage you to go deeper. Is there anyone that can share the blame with you? Is there anyone else you are angry at? It's very important to assign the blame both outside of yourself and inside of yourself—this is what shows you the mirror of your reality so you can feel and understand in your heart your incredible power to change your reality by doing your inner work.

HOW DOES THE WOUND TRACE BACK TO THE 6 CORE WOUNDS?

The six core wounds are Abandonment, Betrayal, Control, Injustice, Rejection, and Shame. Here's a quick overview of each:

- **Control** - A desire to be God or like a god; you want to be the sole creator in your reality or a co-creator in another's reality

- **Abandonment** - Claiming what is not yours by divine design; you are abandoning the truth of who you are

- **Shame** - Judging your higher power's creations, including yourself and others; all of your higher power's creations are perfection

- **Rejection** - Running or hiding from what is yours by divine design; believing in the illusion of your deepest desires running from you

- **Betrayal** - Blaming your higher power's creations for a pattern that exists within you rather than healing it for yourself

- **Injustice** - Believing the illusion of time and space; giving into distorted order or chaos; not believing that things are always expanding into their divine order

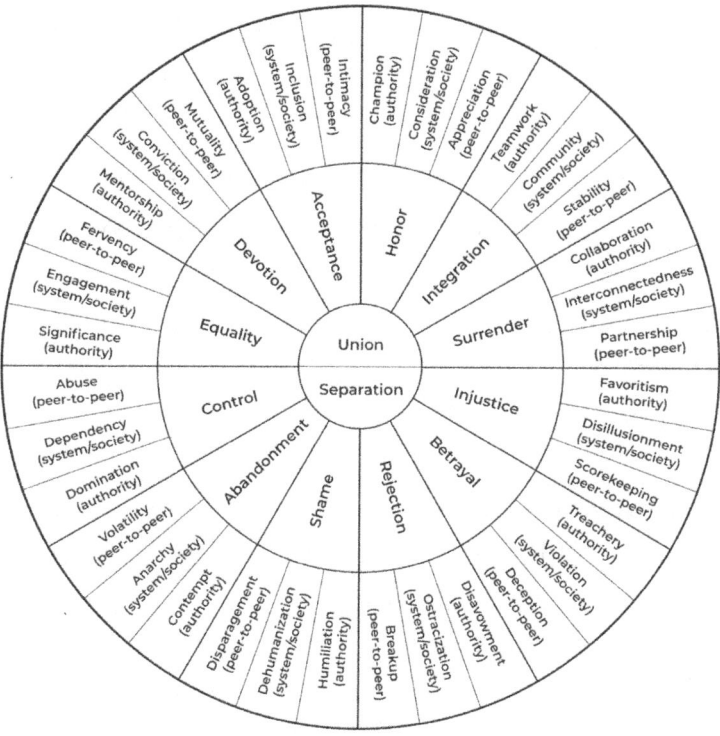

There are two ways you can answer this question:

#1 - You can write out the situation in a sentence or two based on your own intuition. This is the most common way, especially when starting out.

- **Example #1:** "My mother is trying to control my child (and by proxy, me) by bribing him with gifts."

- **Example #2:** "My twin soul won't respond to my messages and I don't know why he's avoiding me."

- **Example #3:** "I'm embarrassed and ashamed by my weight gain and emotional eating."

#2 - You can use the Core Wound Wheel to help identify the thread of the wound more systematically and formally trace it back to one of the six core wounds. For this, you'll want to grab my Core Wound Wheel Cheat Sheet. This tool may give you more specific words or help you trace the wound (and it's emotions and false beliefs) more easily.

- **Example #1:** "My mother is trying to control my child (and by proxy, me), by bribing him with gifts. This triggers my wound around being undermined (specifically, her undermining my authority as a parent) and makes me feel bullied and controlled by her."

- **Example #2:** "My twin soul won't respond to my messages and I don't know why he's avoiding me. This triggers my wounding around abandonment. Specifically with abandonment, I don't know why he responds sometimes and ignores me other times, and I long for consistency and doing it 'right.' Is he ever going to respond to my needs?"

- **Example #3:** "I'm embarrassed and ashamed by my weight gain and emotional eating. I feel like I'm wearing all my problems on my body, where everyone can see them. I worry that people judge me for being 'fat' and devalue my abilities and contributions because I am not stereotypically attractive according to society."

Neither way is better than the other and you can heal without the Core Wound Wheel. If you enjoy speedier results, the Core Wound Wheel is a great tool to have in this process!

STEP 2: IDENTIFYING THE EMOTIONS AROUND THE WOUND

Once you have the basics of the wound, this step is easy because all you have to do is figure out how all of this makes you feel.

A wound with no emotion behind it has no charge and thus isn't likely creating a pattern of behavior in your life. If an event in your life has no emotional charge, you can be fairly sure that it is no longer affecting you and that you have healed it. Emotions are a good indicator if you are wondering how you've progressed in your healing, and healing literally takes the charge and emotion out of the experience so it no longer affects you.

Ask yourself how you feel regarding your upset.

Feel free to write down anything and everything you feel. This will be helpful during clearing.

- **Example #1:** "When my mom bullies and controls me, it makes me feel like she doesn't respect me, like she doesn't see me as a grown-up or my own person, like she doesn't feel happy for me, like she is trying to live vicariously through me rather than support my life, like she is self-centered and selfish..."

- **Example #2:** "When my twin soul ignores me, it feels like he doesn't love me anymore and we are never going to resolve the issues between us. It actually feels like he never loved me—why can't he help me get closure on the questions I'm asking him? Do I mean so little to him that he can't even respond that he's not going to talk to me about this? I feel disrespected, disregarded, and worthless."

- **Example #3:** "When I'm overweight, I feel embarrassed, like a failure, and like a loser who can't stay healthy. I also have additional pain in my body that makes it hard to move, and I struggle to do any sort of exercise to help myself. I feel hopeless that I can ever be small or a normal weight again. And this just makes me want to eat more, which starts the cycle again."

STEP 3: IDENTIFYING THE BELIEF YOU'VE FORMED AROUND THE WOUND

Now you have both the logical or facts-based issues of the upset as well as the emotional issues of the upset. How have these created a belief inside you that serves as the narrative of this pattern you are in with this person or situation? You can figure this out by stating what you believe about the situation.

- **Example #1:** I believe:

    - That if my mother buys my child gifts she is trying to bribe him to control him

    - That when my mother takes action I don't approve of, it undermines my authority

    - That my mother is taking action to circumvent my authority and gain control over my child

    - That my mother doesn't respect my authority

    - That my mother is all about herself and doesn't respect that this is my child, my experience, my life, my rules

    - And so on...

- **Example #2:** I believe:

  - That if he doesn't text me back it's personal

  - That he doesn't want to have the conversation that I'm trying to have with him

  - That the love isn't there

  - That I'm too boring to him and not even worth his attention

  - That there's zero respect to give me an answer or at least say there won't be an answer

  - And so on...

- **Example #3:** I believe:

  - That not being able to lose weight is an indication of success as a person

  - That my value is wrapped up in what I look like

  - That I'm losing opportunities or otherwise failing at something when I present myself as overweight

  - That I'm being judged when I talk to others who are much skinnier than me

  - That I'm not attractive anymore and

therefore invisible to others

- That I look terrible in pictures and should be embarrassed to do normal life things like dress up or be in photos at a birthday party

- And so on...

PHASE 2: UPROOT

The next phase of healing is to uproot all the false beliefs that are holding you in a deep pattern of wounding. *A Course in Miracles* states, "If you heal the beliefs about your wounds then you heal the wounds themselves. The wounds no longer hold any power over you." Your core wounding always centers around false beliefs; when you identify and accept the truth, you are healed and this pattern that no longer serves you can no longer rule your life.

To do this, we'll flip the rock up on your beliefs, unhook you from the stories that you've told yourself, and eradicate these patterns from your thoughts.

STEP 1: QUESTION YOUR BELIEFS

For the purposes of healing, we can assume that all beliefs are actually false. Why? The beliefs are creating a pattern that is disrupting your peace, and anything that disrupts your peace is out of alignment with your higher power and makes you feel bad.

Even if you pegged the other person's motives perfectly, what is the point in believing the story you've told yourself? Whether false or true, you want to change the pattern, right?

This is not about becoming a doormat to the other person, either. You may be completely correct about the story, but there's still a huge illusion to the story, and that's rooted in this person being an innocent, a child under your higher power, just as you are. The story is an illusion no matter what because it is created from wounding. Even if you "get it right" you are still viewing that other person through the lens of fear, scarcity, control, anger, and ego, which is all an illusion.

In order to restore peace, you must assume that your beliefs are false. If the beliefs are false, you want to correct them in your thoughts and rewire your brain with the truth.

You can do this by flipping all the beliefs on their heads via the mirror. To use the mirror, simply take anything the other person is doing and attribute it to yourself in addition to them.

Example #1:

- I believe that if my mother buys my child gifts she is trying to bribe him to control him → I am controlling what flows to my child because I want to control him

- I believe that when my mother takes action I don't approve of, it undermines my authority → I am undermining my own authority by allowing my mother to take actions I don't approve of

- I believe that my mother is taking action to circumvent my authority and gain control over my child → I am taking (or not taking) action to circumvent my authority and gain control over my child

- I believe that my mother doesn't respect my authority → I don't respect my authority over my child enough to say a hard and firm no to the gifts

- I believe that my mother is all about herself and doesn't respect that this is my child, my experience, my life, my rules → I am focused on myself and my own experience and not allowing my mother to enjoy hers

When I force myself to flip the rock on these beliefs, I see that I have co-created this pattern. My mom is simply reflecting back to me my own lack of authority. If I believe she has control and authority over my child, I believe I don't hold full control and authority over my child.

As the parent and legal guardian of the child, I make all the rules and decisions for my child. Everyone else earns access to my child through my trust. This is supported by both my country's legal system and by society, as healthy access to *any* child is earned through earning the trust of their parents first.

I further see that I have been conflict-avoidant about the issue and have not given a firm "no" regarding what I do and do not accept in this relationship. I am allowing myself to be undermined, bullied, and controlled by not setting appropriate boundaries and having the conversation right then and there.

Example #2:

- I believe that if he doesn't text me back it's personal → I believe when I don't have my stuff together people take it personally

- I believe that he doesn't want to have the conversation that I'm trying to have with him → I don't want to have the conversation with myself or by myself and am looking for someone outside of me to give me my peace

- I believe that the love isn't there → I'm not loving myself around this situation

- I believe that I'm too boring to him and not even worth his attention → I'm bored with myself unless I'm getting attention outside of myself and feel worthless on my own

- I believe that there's zero respect to give me an answer or at least say there won't be an answer → I am disrespectful toward myself and not giving myself the closure I want and need

When I flip the rock on these beliefs, I see that I'm seeking love, attention, and closure outside of myself. I long to have this conversation with someone else in order to stir up drama because I'm ultimately bored with thinking about it and processing it on my own. And I'm staying in a place of unrest instead of giving myself the peace and love I desire, now. I'm tying my respect of self to another and their actions, when I truly know that I'm worthy of a response and that not receiving one has everything to do with the other person's respect issues, not mine.

Going deeper, because this is my twin soul, if I give myself the love and attention I desire, my twin soul will reflect that. If I've truly healed this wound completely, I can look around at my life to see where this healing is reflected.

Example #3:

- I believe that not being able to lose weight is an indication of success as a person → I judge success based on superficial and irrelevant factors

- I believe that my value is wrapped up in what I look like → I'm judging others' value on their looks when I know that people have inherent value

- I believe that I'm losing opportunities or otherwise failing at something when I present myself as overweight → I take away others' opportunities and consider them failures if they are overweight

- I believe that I'm being judged when I talk to others who are much skinnier than me → I am judging a skinny person by their body when talking to them

- I believe that I'm not attractive anymore and therefore invisible to others → I find myself unattractive and thus I'm making myself invisible (not being seen or heard)

- I believe that I look terrible in pictures and should be embarrassed to do normal life things like dress up or be in photos at a birthday party → I don't believe that I should be able to have a normal life until I lose weight

When I flip the rock on these beliefs, I see that I am majorly judging others based on their looks and ability to manage their weight! In the past, I would be blaming and shaming myself for this, but I can find relief in identifying the root of my upset because I know the perfect process for healing it. I also see that I find myself unattractive and I'm holding myself back in all areas of my life because I'm not willing to be seen at my current weight.

I know from experience that there is no amount of "skinny" or "attractive" that will put me at peace until I do the inner work. With a relationship, there's no amount of love or attention that someone can give you to satiate your desire if you are not giving love and attention to yourself. This is because they can be giving you all the love and attention in the world but you are unable to truly receive it until you heal the patterns within.

The same is true for my supposed weight issues. The issue is not my weight—that's just a symbol of the issue. The issue is instead around loving myself, understanding my worthiness to receive love no matter what my body looks like, and building my attractiveness with myself.

In this case, it's really important to understand that I'm not saying to myself, "okay, eat whatever you want, don't exercise, don't try to lose weight because it doesn't matter." Loving yourself and building your attractiveness to yourself may still mean making changes to your personal habits, but it must come from a place of love rather than a place of shame, bullying, or criticizing yourself.

STEP 2: UNHOOK YOURSELF FROM THE STORY OF THE BELIEF

We have changed the false belief at the thought

level, and now we will change it at the emotional level by rewiring our hearts. This is largely done through letting go of the story we told ourselves, as emotions are expressed through story rather than fact.

First, come to a place within where you are open to the truth of the situation. With compassion for yourself and a commitment to not blame or shame yourself, consider these questions:

- Am I contributing to the situation?

- Is the conclusion of my emotions true?

- Is there contrary evidence to my beliefs?

- If I put myself in the other person's shoes, is there another motive or intention I can find here?

- Is there another story the other person's actions and behaviors could support?

Example #1:

- **Am I contributing to the situation?** Is it that my mom doesn't respect my authority over my child or is it that I'm not standing up for myself and seizing the authority I know is mine by social and legal right?

- **Is the conclusion of my emotions true?** Does my mom really not see me as a grown-up, or does she have different motivations for her behavior that have nothing to do with me? Do I see myself as a grown up, or do I have work to do there?

- **Is there contrary evidence to my beliefs?** Has my mom bribed others for love? Is her generosity a bribe?

- **If I put myself in the other person's shoes, is there another motive or intention I can find here?** Does my mom have her own wounding that could be driving her intentions, or does my mom have a healing that I have not yet attained?

- **Is there another story the other person's actions and behaviors could support?** Does my mom want to give this gift for another reason besides control and undermining me?

The story I was telling myself was very personal; this step helps to depersonalize and thus decharge my emotions around the situation. Most things others do to us are not personal and have to do with their own motivations or their own wounding. When we can depersonalize the emotions, we can move toward compassion for the other person.

The questions show me that there are a lot of reasons this is happening and that I don't have to attribute malice to my mom. She is most likely excited about building a relationship with her grandchild and wants to shower him with gifts to show her love. At the end of the day, we may have a conflict of values over this issue but neither set of values is wrong or bad.

Example #2:

- **Am I contributing to the situation?** Is it really compassionate to keep asking my twin soul the same questions over and over again? Especially when they've been asked and not answered in the past? Do I trust that my twin soul (and God) has a reason for not sharing what's on his mind around this particular subject for the moment?

- **Is the conclusion of my emotions true?** Does my twin soul not love me or are they overwhelmed right now? They are responding to me, just not on that topic, so maybe it's the topic and not me.

- **Is there contrary evidence to my beliefs?** Has my twin soul ignored me before? What was the reasoning behind it? Did I learn something later that helped me understand?

- **If I put myself in the other person's shoes, is there another motive or intention I can find here?** Does my twin soul have his own wounding that could be driving him, or is he placing a boundary for a reason?

- **Is there another story the other person's actions and behaviors could support?** Is he ignoring me for a reason that has nothing to do with his love for me?

The story I was telling myself about my twin soul is that everything needed to be on the table with him because he is my twin soul. I didn't understand why he wouldn't talk to me about something very personal, when really he is still a human, twin soul or not. Connections between humans, including your twin soul, have to be built and earned. He doesn't owe me responses to my very personal questions, even if he intends to tell me the truth eventually. It may not be the right time or he may not have any more to share about it for now. In the past, he has also demonstrated that he prefers to process things by himself, in his own head, and when he does finally come to a conclusion, he tends to let me know.

There was also a question of, am I getting ghosted or is it a brush-off? Is my twin soul lying to me to get me off their back? But in truth, my twin soul has never demonstrated lying to me—that is my wounding from a different relationship where everything was a lie. I can take everything shared with me at face value and the lack of communication is likely not malicious, but rather not having the words to communicate and not wanting to lie or brush off the situation. If my twin soul didn't want to talk to me about it ever again, I think he would confront the issue and say so, so there must be a timing reason for why he isn't sharing what's going on.

Example #3:

- **Am I contributing to the situation?** I feel judged for my weight because I'm judging myself for my weight. And so far, bullying myself into submission around eating and exercise isn't working! If I truly want to make changes, why not approach weight loss from a place of love, and by partnering with my higher power?

- **Is the conclusion of my emotions true?** Are there people who don't use weight as an indicator of success or one having their life together? Lots of people are extremely successful in many areas of their life, like business, and also struggle with weight issues. Am I conflating two separate things?

- **Is there contrary evidence to my beliefs?** Am I "successful" despite having extra weight? How do I define success, and can't I define it any way I want?

- **If I put myself in the other person's shoes, is there another motive or intention I can find**

here? What is my true intention for making my weight a blocker for being seen? Is it safer to hide than to put myself out there with my divine purpose and creative projects?

- **Is there another story the other person's actions and behaviors could support?** Am I using my weight as an excuse to not be successful in other areas of my life?

The story I was telling myself about my weight was that I needed to lose weight to succeed in business. I ultimately believed that my "brand" wasn't attractive enough because I wasn't young, pretty, and thin. I was triggered when I saw other women who fit these standards growing their businesses quickly, and was attributing their success to, "well, she's skinnier than me."

In truth, I also admired dozens of women who didn't have the stereotypically "hot" or "attractive" body type and I hadn't given their weight a second thought when considering working with them. Weight was not actually holding them back from the success they wanted, and it wasn't holding me back either.

I also decided that I did want to lose weight, but that it was entirely for myself and not a blocker to loving myself as I am now. I had in the past come at my weight loss from a place of abusing myself, but I knew I could find an incredibly loving path to losing weight with God and my healing work.

STEP 3: UPROOT AND ERADICATE THE BELIEF

Now that the emotions have less charge, it's easy to step back into the thought process and eradicate this belief from my system so it no longer controls my actions and reactions.

Example #1: My mom can't undermine me unless I let her.

The pattern is, she says she is going to take action that crosses my boundaries as a parent; I nod in the moment and stew for months in silence about it, never confronting the issue head-on; she knows nothing of my frustration, distrust, and anger at her and continues to cross my boundaries (because of course this is not about gifts—the gifts are just a symbol. It's instead about what those gifts represent in my mind).

A healthy response is to address the situation directly and let her know I would prefer she doesn't buy gifts because it doesn't jive with my core value of teaching my child to be financially independent as an adult. I also do not want my child to associate money or gifts with love as not everyone in his life has the money to shower him with gifts. Finally, I do not want a situation where my child feels he has to maintain a connection with someone or he will not receive an inheritance later—that is sure to cause wounding and trauma that I wish to avoid.

I can further be clear that this is my decision and my rule. I can share that taking action on this behind my back would cause distrust in me, and I cannot leave my child alone with someone I distrust.

Example #2: My twin soul is not ready to talk about this situation, so there must be somewhere inside me that also isn't ready to talk about the situation.

The pattern is, I come to him pretending to want to connect, he tries to talk to me, and I pull the rug out from under him with my prodding questions and insistence on a specific discussion in order to continue. I believed that it was him that didn't want to connect, but actually it's also me, as he has tried to connect with me and I've made it clear that I will not connect until he answers my questions. I believed it was him that wasn't loving me, but also it's me not loving him and his process for dealing with the situation in his own way, on his own terms. I believed that he was putting up the blockers to our relationship, but also I was issuing unspoken ultimatums, essentially saying, we can't be in a relationship or friendship until you answer my questions.

Example #3: I truly desire to lose weight in my own time and through my own process, wanting only to do it from a place of love.

At the same time, I'm beating myself up for not

getting fast-track results on my weight loss, even though I don't want to fast-track my efforts. A little compassion is needed here, as I am never truly in disagreement with myself. The larger pattern is that I prefer to take things at a slow pace and go deep on my issues because I want to heal things permanently. I'm tired of making short-term changes and getting ephemeral results. Going deeper takes time, and the outward results are slower, but I ultimately believe that I am on the fast-track because I'm healing permanently.

PHASE 3: UNMASK

There is a spiritual meme centered around the comically clichéd ending to every Scooby Doo episode. The gang catches the villain and explains the mystery and all the clues they spotted to figure it out. Then, they unmask the villain, who is almost always in a silly costume.

In this spiritual meme, the gang unmasks the villain and it turns out to be the person doing the unmasking! In this phase, we unmask ourselves as the "villain" of the show. I say this in jest, of course—do not enter a blame and shame spiral as you reveal yourself as the person behind the mask. The purpose of this phase is to take the healing much deeper so that you never have to experience the same trigger or upset through contrast again.

At this point, you may already be feeling some peace or completion with the situation. After all, you have come to a place of compassion for the person, discharged the icky feelings around the situation, and rewired both your heart and mind toward new, more supportive beliefs.

Yet, it's important to keep going through the process. If you stop in the middle, you won't truly change the belief and thus you won't achieve permanent peace around this belief. That's because thus far, we have only examined false beliefs around a specific situation. The true healing is going to come from using one situation to heal multiple situations; otherwise, your wounding around this will come up again.

Step 1: Find the Larger Truth of the Situation

Have you heard the saying, "the way you do one thing is the way you do everything?" While I do think you can have massive success in one area of your life while struggling in others, I also believe that the same patterns show up over and over again everywhere in your life. This makes sense because the root cause of those patterns is always wounding.

Some questions you can ask yourself are:

- What societal influences caused this situation?

- What childhood wounds did I experience or re-experience with this situation? What about the other person? (You can trace theirs back too in many cases!)

- What general patterns do I or they fall into that may have caused this situation?

A big part of the twin soul and ascension journey is to notice that every conflict you have with another human being, including your twin soul, is merely an interaction of your mutual wounding, With others, the wounding patterns are often complimentary, but it's easy for one or both of you to break the pattern through recognizing healthy boundaries or taking time apart. With your twin soul, the wounding patterns are the same and within both of you, making the triggers feel larger and the matching pattern within harder for you to recognize and heal.

- **Example #1:** With this situation, I was attributing gifts, generosity, and excitement to control, undermining, and taking away my authority. I also have a people-pleasing wound around receiving gifts in exchange for something. Many others would not have a tit-for-tat hangup or believe that they need to engage in a relationship in order to receive a gift.

- **Example #2:** I have a habit of insisting I'm right or my way is the right way with everyone and everything. In my mind, the step-by-step of building this connection with my twin soul is to clear out the elephants in the room, then take the next step (becoming friends or having a relationship). I'm goal-oriented and systematic. But he tends to prefer building things organically and hates to force situations forward. He relies more on intuition, feeling, and letting the connection or relationship unfold in its perfect timing.

- **Example #3:** As a young child I was taught that being overweight was an indication of failure across all areas of life. One of my worst fears was being overweight, and I am still in shock that I ever let myself get overweight to begin with. I have spent years projecting this challenge in my life onto everyone and everything, pointing the problem to outside of myself. I have spent time beating myself up for it too. I've also had a number of false beliefs about my weight over the years, like that I don't lose weight easily or I can't control my weight.

STEP 2: FIND THE PATTERN IN THE TWIN SOUL TRINITY

Every false belief leads back to yourself or your creator—your higher power, God, Spirit, Source, Mother Nature, the Universe, and so on.

You could take the wounding all the way back to

these true sources alone, but because this is specifically a book about uniting with your twin soul, I will use the Twin Soul Trinity to take us all the way back to the point of creation for this wound.

For me, once I see that this is a pattern in my life, I truly know that it's mine to heal and I get very excited. After all, I can heal the pattern and completely eradicate dozens of situations that caused past pain—that's incredible! I love uncovering these patterns because I know that I'm about to release a big piece of separation from my twin soul and my union.

I like to take things all the way back to the Twin Soul Trinity because we are on the twin soul journey and we are here to do twin soul work! If you heal a pattern anywhere in your life, you can see it reflected in your twin soul union. It helps to connect the dots so that this is more obvious to you immediately.

Ask yourself:

- Where do I see this pattern in myself?

- Where do I see this pattern in my relationship with my twin soul?

- Where do I see this pattern in my relationship with my higher power?

- Where do I see this pattern in my relationship with others?

Example #1

- **Myself:** I don't give myself gifts or rewards,

not even for completing work. If I have any free time, I fill it with more work and tasks. I also feel uncomfortable with receiving gifts and opening them in front of others. It feels like I'm taking something I don't deserve, which is crazy!

- **My twin soul:** When my twin soul does something sweet for me, I immediately feel guilty. This is strange because Acts of Service is my love language and I truly love when others shower me with help, assistance, and support in my daily life. At the same time, I feel resentful when I have to do so much for others and deplete my cup as a result, so I assume that everyone else gets resentful when they give too.

- **My higher power:** It's hard for me to receive my love and good from God. I struggle to receive money from doing my divine purpose, which I would do anyway. I struggle to accept compliments from others. Receiving love in general makes me uncomfortable.

- **Others:** I have had suspicion and distrust around gifts and people bribing me with gifts, from a situation with my dad to a situation with an ex-boyfriend. I have assumed that people give gifts to pacify others and escape any real connection.

Example #2:

- **Myself:** I have a tendency to harass myself and force myself to deal with things. My motto is, "get it over with," and that doesn't always produce the best experience. I can be impatient with myself sometimes as well, and I sometimes make rash decisions by communicating something that's not ready to be communicated.

- **My twin soul:** I was pushing my twin soul in places he wasn't ready to communicate. I have done this often and frequently pushed him to move forward on something that I had decided we needed to move forward on. When he wasn't ready, I made it a big drama instead of giving him time to come into his own decision about it. I questioned our relationship just because the timing was off or we were coming at decisions from two different processes.

- **My higher power:** I've been demanding of life in the past and had to relax more as I've gotten older. Life is meant to be enjoyed, rather than to be rushed through or worked through.

- **Others:** I do like to be right with others as well, and I often think that my way is the best way or the way that makes the most sense, when other people have their own processes.

Example #3:

- **Myself:** I sometimes still beat myself up for not choosing divinely, and choosing distorted order or chaos instead. When I changed from my 6-figure career to my divine purpose, it also took a lot of time to rebuild and rethink how I worked. At the time I beat myself up for "starting so late," but now that I'm older I'm deeply proud of how much courage I actually had to go against everything I was taught about success. Weight loss can be the same for me; I'm not too late, I'm actually early in desiring to give my body deep care and love. It will take time to learn a new way but choosing my own divinity is inevitable, natural, and easy. I don't truly need to lose weight in the typical fashion; my weight loss will easily unfold over time through healing.

- **My twin soul:** My relationship with my twin soul unfolds easily through healing as well. I never need to exert a ton of effort to build our connection. I only need to heal and the connection will unfold naturally and intuitively.

- **My higher power:** I sometimes feel like I need to "connect" with God more aggressively. I think to myself, "I'm not healing fast enough," or "I'm not spiritual enough," because I don't use my tarot cards or meditate every day. But my connection with God grows naturally because I am interacting with him through all parts of my life. It is impossible not to commune with him; he is literally everywhere, in everything and everyone.

- **Others:** I get frustrated with others for not healing fast enough too! I see their obvious wounding and pressure them to heal it faster. Really, it's none of my business, I don't truly care (aside from my desire to be right), and they are on their own spiritual and healing journeys.

STEP 3: ENTER THE HEALING PROCESS SINCERELY

Compassion is critical to healing the pattern, and for this I highly recommend the Ho'oponopono Method, also known as the Forgiveness exercise. "Ho'oponopono" roughly translates to, "make it right," and this is what we will do around this pattern. You can write out your Ho'oponopono method for every piece of the pattern you've unmasked, including the original situation, how this false belief has played out with others, and how this false belief has played out in the Twin Soul Trinity. I have also found that looking at this only with your higher power works well too as this is truly the point of creation for the wounding. Healing at the point of creation will heal it forward as well in a domino effect.

The four parts of this exercise are:

- I'm sorry

- Please forgive me

- Thank you

- I love you

Example #1:

- I'm sorry for not receiving your gifts.

- Please forgive me for thinking you were manipulating me.

- Thank you for your love for me.

- I love you for wanting to give me love.

Example #2:

- I'm sorry I'm not connecting with you.

- Please forgive me for pushing my own agenda and not listening.

- Thank you for your desire to connect with me.

- I love you as you are and find your processes toward life extremely interesting.

Example #3:

- I'm sorry that I've bullied, shamed and abused your creation (me!) for so many years.

- Please forgive me for not taking care of your child and loving her as she should have been loved.

- Thank you for your unending patience and guidance as I learn to love this body the way you intended.

- I love you for giving me this body and this life on earth, as it's the ultimate gift.

PHASE 4: UNION

Now that you've truly gone through the process of releasing this pattern from your reality permanently, you can easily come back into union with yourself in this area.

STEP 1: MAKE A NEW CHOICE

You have done a lot of work around rewiring your brain and your heart. This step encourages you to make a declaration of what you truly desire instead of your old patterns. You can write this out, but it's far more important to feel your new truth moving through your body. As you read back what you've written (or as you meditate on your new choice), you can visualize the intention moving through your body from head to toe, transforming every cell as it moves. You will know you are aligned to your new choice when you feel a wave of peace washing over you.

You may also experience feelings of stress or anxiety. This is only an indication that there is more healing to do on this wound. That anxiety is literally the feeling of some of the cells in your body continuing to believe in and support the false beliefs that held you in the pattern to begin with. But don't worry about it or start beating yourself up for not ridding yourself of every last bit of the wounding.

You can heal this now by going back to Phases 1-3, or you can let it go for now and trust that it will come back up later for healing. I have found that sometimes it makes sense to go back and find additional threads, while other times I am just trying to force myself into an analytical healing that just leaves me spinning and frustrated. Either way, the feeling of peace is what you're looking for. It doesn't need to be complete to feel good, so accept the level of peace you receive now and know that more is coming soon.

Example #1: I can see that I struggle to receive abundance from others and attribute it to a desire to control or placate me.

I choose instead to open myself to all abundance

and understand that there is no tit-for-tat. I can receive anything offered to me without owing anyone anything. I trust myself to discern when someone is offering something from a place of love versus a place of fear. I trust myself to place healthy boundaries around my own people-pleasing behaviors. I open myself to receiving gifts from God through any means possible.

Example #2: I can see that I'm rooted in control and ego around my communication with others.

I choose instead to release my need for the step-by-step process that I think is right, or the timing that I think is right. It's safe to let the steps unfold naturally, and I can handle and respond gracefully to anything that comes up "out of order." I realize that I tend to get ahead of myself and talk at people, rather than listen to them, too. I'm so sure of where things are going that I can't handle surprises or people revealing themselves to me in a way that doesn't fit my original narrative. I also try to go deep too quickly in some cases.

Example #3: I can see that I desire to move through life slowly rather than forcing quick change or quick results.

Moving through life slowly means that sometimes the physical results will come over the long-term rather than the short term. This doesn't matter—the physical world is an illusion—and doing life slowly is actually the fast-track, because I'm healing things permanently rather than trying to take a shortcut or chase a temporary high.

STEP 2: RELEASE EVERYTHING NOT ALIGNED TO THE NEW CHOICE

As you move through your life in the minutes and hours following a clearing and healing, you may find yourself holding onto a false belief or wounding out of habit. You'll know that it's out of habit and not out of lack of healing because you find yourself going there mindlessly, but no longer feel any emotion around it. I found this when I broke my addiction to numbing out with alcohol. I could drink or not drink, it really didn't matter to me emotionally. But I ordered a drink sometimes merely out of habit. I could easily order a mocktail or a glass of water instead, and it didn't have any emotional charge for me one way or the other, because I had attained peace.

You may notice this in yourself, and you can simply guide yourself back to peace. If you are struggling to guide yourself back, you may want to go through the 5U Healing Process or the Reflection Journaling Practice again, handling anything that is currently coming up for you.

I find it helpful to have a one-liner to remind myself of the truth I've discovered. For example, when I go back to a place of regret, I remind myself, "My journey is perfect for me." When I go back to a place of feeling like I'll never be forgiven, I remind myself, "I am not the source of my twin soul's pain." These one-liners are things I truly believe, but having the words helps to bring me back to peace immediately.

Example #1:

- "I can receive without going into debt."

- "A gift brings the giver as much pleasure as the recipient."

Example #2:

- "I don't need to be right right now."

- "Let's make a small effort and see what unfolds from there."

- "'Hello' is a complete sentence and a perfect launching pad for something deeper."

Example #3:

- "I'm healing this permanently which is why it's taking longer than I or others expect."

- "No shortcuts! Take the time to heal it for good."

- "I'm loving myself by taking my time with this."

STEP 3: ALIGN TO THE NEW CHOICE

You can stay in your new belief and healing by supporting yourself through your actions. Don't overthink this or create grand plans. Instead, simply notice areas in your life where you could support your new choice.

- **Example #1:** The next time my mom offers my child or myself money, I can say, "Sure, thanks." It really doesn't have to be a thing!

- **Example #2:** The next time my twin soul wants to communicate something, I'll let the conversation unfold naturally and spend more time listening than talking. I trust that he desires to connect and I don't need to control the situation.

- **Example #3:** The next time I eat, I will only desire to eat with God, as there is a divine amount of food I'm meant to consume, along with divine cravings that help me understand what nutrients my body needs.

PHASE 5: UPHEAVAL

The last phase of healing is one that will unfold over the weeks and months to follow, especially if you have had a big healing cycle. There are no steps to the Upheaval phase, but there are some things you may experience that are normal and natural. If you don't realize that they are a part of upheaval, however, it could feel like you are experiencing disaster and failure in your reality.

Nothing could be further from the truth. As long as you are moving toward your true self and your higher power, you are moving forward, not backward.

#1 - CONNECTING THE DOTS OF YOUR PAST EXPERIENCES

You have released your old story, so it's natural and expected that you would write a new story. You may notice patterns and have insights about why something unfolded the way it did. Through healing, you have taken dots that were once connected in a certain way and erased those connections. Naturally, you will rearrange the dots and build new, peaceful, and supportive stories.

#2 - RELEASING PEOPLE, PLACES, SITUATIONS, AND EXPERIENCES

You may notice that you are causing more conflict in your old life. Perhaps you are getting into more fights with your loved ones, or you are putting up with less abuse at work. This is normal because you have released an old vibration through your healing. Your reality is going to shift around you, slowly, as the physical realm is more dense than the spiritual realm where you completed your healing. People, places, and more are going to vibrate out of your reality.

#3 - MOURNING YOUR OLD SELF

Just because you want the ending and know the ending is coming, doesn't mean you won't mourn it. Expect a mix of emotions as you heal. It's much like graduating high school. You are both dying to get out and shocked and sad that it's all over. You are both excited for college or moving out and scared that you are on your own now.

You are still human and it's okay and normal to hold mixed emotions over receiving what you desire.

In addition to mourning your old self, you may find aspects of your true self that surprise you. This is usually a welcome surprise, but it can also be jarring when you've invested years or even decades of your life believing something about who you are. The ascension process is literally a journey back to your true self, and discovering your twin soul is also about unveiling yourself so you can recognize them properly. Be open to surprises about who you are, and realize that these unveilings are not meant to upset you, they are meant to reunite you with yourself. It's a beautiful gift to receive from your higher power!

#4 - RE-TRIGGERING AND REPROCESSING THE ONION LAYERS OF THE WOUND

Even though you've healed your current wounding, you may find that the wounding comes back around, a bit like water circling a drain. The truth is that we heal in a spiral rather than a straight line. The spiral takes us deeper to new layers of the same wounding.

It's common to feel frustrated by this, but I encourage you instead to be at peace with the process and let things play out naturally. Wounds leave echoes, reverberating backwards and forwards through the timeline of your life/lives. Upheaval is feeling these wounds as you are editing and rewriting your story.

I have found that when I am re-triggered, the pain is less like a punch to the gut and more like a bee sting, or eventually, a pin prick. There is a thread of something there, but it's not a tower collapsing around me like it was before.

My drawing teacher once told me that it doesn't matter if I spill water across my artwork. If I could draw it once, I can draw it again. This is a sign of mastery over a domain, when nothing can truly damage or disturb your peace. This is how you know your work is permanent.

So I will say the same to you. Seeing the same trigger pop up again is nothing to fear. And if you healed it before, you can heal it again.

JOURNALING PROMPTS

- What do you think of the 5U Healing Process? What parts do you recognize or use already? What new ideas did you learn from it?

- How could you apply the 5U Healing Process to your favorite healing modality or modalities?

- How could you simplify the 5U Healing Process to make it something that you can remember easily? How could you take the 5U Healing Process "on the go" so that it's easy enough to do in your head?

FEELING STUCK?

- **Download the 5U Healing Process Cheat Sheet.** You can post this on your wall or in your journal or planner so you have the process with you and easily accessible at all times. You can also grab my printable on turning the 5U Healing Process into your preferred healing modality, so that you can create a unique meditation, tarot spread, astrology reading, and more. Learn more about the 5U Healing Process here: http://cardreadingqueen.com/5u

- **Check out the Core Wound Wheel Cheat Sheet** which helps you identify and name the wounding you are experiencing now. This can be extremely helpful in getting you to stop numbing out to potential separation consciousness that is holding you back from your union. Get the cheat sheet at http://card-readingqueen.com/core-wound-wheel/

Chapter Eleven
THE REFLECTION JOURNALING PRACTICE

I f you want to use the 5U Healing Process for all of your healing needs, you will uncover a great deal of understanding about why your healing and wounding has unfolded as it has. But that is not always practical when you are healing minor challenges in your life or healing multiple upsets per day.

Because I cannot tolerate my own upsets for long, and because I choose to have my peace now, I also use a quick shorthand called the Reflection Journaling Practice if I'm trying to get to the root of my healing quickly. This practice is easy to do once you are familiar with the 5U Healing Process of healing. What I've done is condensed the 5U Healing Process down into a quick and simple journaling exercise where several of the steps are simplified, combined, or skipped over. This works well for minor challenges or areas where I've already done a lot of

healing work and I'm just cleaning up some false beliefs or old wounding. If the Reflection Journaling
Practice is not bringing me peace, or if I'm stuck on
a problem for several days, I will sit down and use
the 5U Healing Process as it is a more robust tool
for truly releasing my wounding completely.

I sometimes do the entire Reflection Journaling
Practice in my head, but I also try to write it out on
paper when needed. I find the visualization extremely helpful to quickly cut through my upsets in re-
al-time, so that I'm consistently healing rather than
saving all my upsets for a long journaling session. I
usually don't even need to complete all the spaces
for the whole Reflection Journaling Practice to find
peace with my current challenge, block, or upset.
Use as much or as little of this tool as you want and
feel free to adapt it to your own style.

STEP #1 - THE UPSET

This is the place where you write out exactly what
is upsetting you. Feel free to use as much space as
you want to describe your upset. You may end up
with multiple threads of the upset to heal, but that's
okay if you take it one thread at a time.

If your upset is really short, sweet, and simple, feel
free to skip Step #1 because the next step, The Mirror, handles the upset already. I've included this step
here, however, for people who are just beginning to

use the tool. As a math nerd and visual artist, I also love the symmetry of the Reflection Journaling Practice starting with Step #1, space #1, and building from there. And finally, I think this step can be practical if you are feeling a litany of sub-upsets around your main upset. You can mindmap from the main circle to really dig into your upsets in more detail.

This step roughly corresponds with the first phase of the 5U Healing Process called Upset.

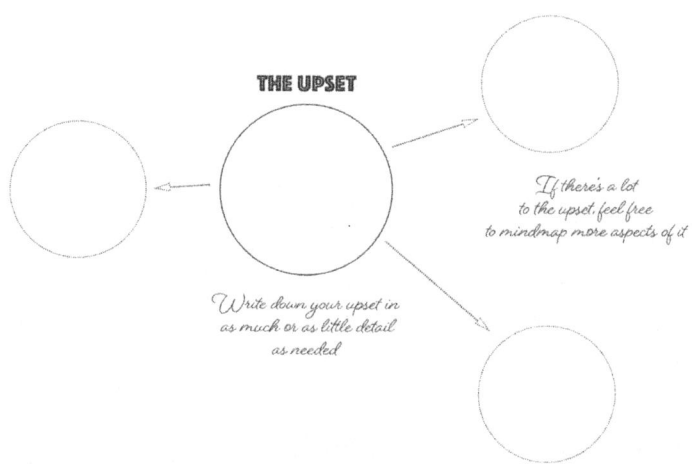

THE UPSET

If there's a lot to the upset, feel free to mindmap more aspects of it

Write down your upset in as much or as little detail as needed

STEP #2 - THE MIRROR

I turn the upset into both sides of the equation, because I believe it's important to both get very real about my human blame and notice where I feel shame within, usually over my true feelings. The mirror visualization reminds me that my inner world creates my outer reality, and that anything I see that I don't like is a pattern within myself.

This step roughly corresponds with the second phase of the 5U Healing Process called Uproot.

THE MIRROR

THE OTHER PERSON   **YOU**

What did they do to you?   *Where do you see the pattern inside yourself?*

STEP #3 - THE POINT OF CREATION

Because this book is about your twin soul journey, and because I am personally on a twin soul journey, I always take my upset back to the Twin Soul Trinity. My purpose for healing is to reunite with my twin soul at every space in my being, so this makes the most sense for me at this time. You can replace this section with anything else you desire to get at the point of creation of your wounding, as long as it helps you see where you are creating separation between you and your twin soul and your higher power.

This step roughly corresponds with the third phase of the 5U Healing Process called Unmask.

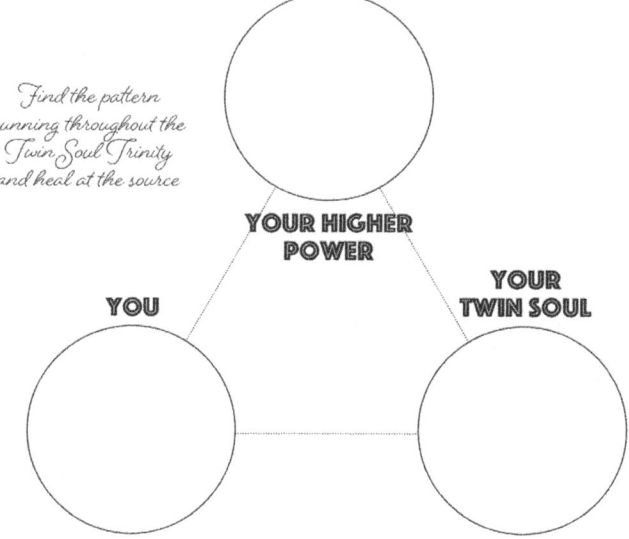

THE TWIN SOUL TRINITY

Find the pattern running throughout the Twin Soul Trinity and heal at the source

YOUR HIGHER POWER

YOU

YOUR TWIN SOUL

STEP #4 - THE HEALING

I use the Ho'oponopono Method or the Forgiveness Exercise to complete my healing. I typically focus on my higher power, God, for this exercise, but sometimes I venture into the healing with my twin soul, or with the person with whom I had the original upset with. I focus on God because I know that if I heal with my higher power, it will ripple out to every other relationship in my life. I like efficiency!

This step roughly corresponds with the fourth phase of the 5U Healing Process called Union.

THE HO'OPONOPONO METHOD

I'M SORRY...

PLEASE FORGIVE ME...

Find forgiveness and compassion for all involved in the situation, including yourself

THANK YOU...

I LOVE YOU...

STEP #5 - WAVE OF PEACE

It helps me to write down my old pattern, then my new pattern so I can visualize the shift I have made through my healing. I also write down three "feel goods" that help me ground my new pattern into reality. I often make these clever one-liners so I can refer back to them when I encounter the old pattern again. And because I love layouts, I form a peace sign with my spaces.

This step also roughly corresponds with the four phase fo the 5U Healing Process called Union. I use this step to recommit to my healing so that when the Upheaval Phase comes, I have strong reminders of the new choice I've committed to.

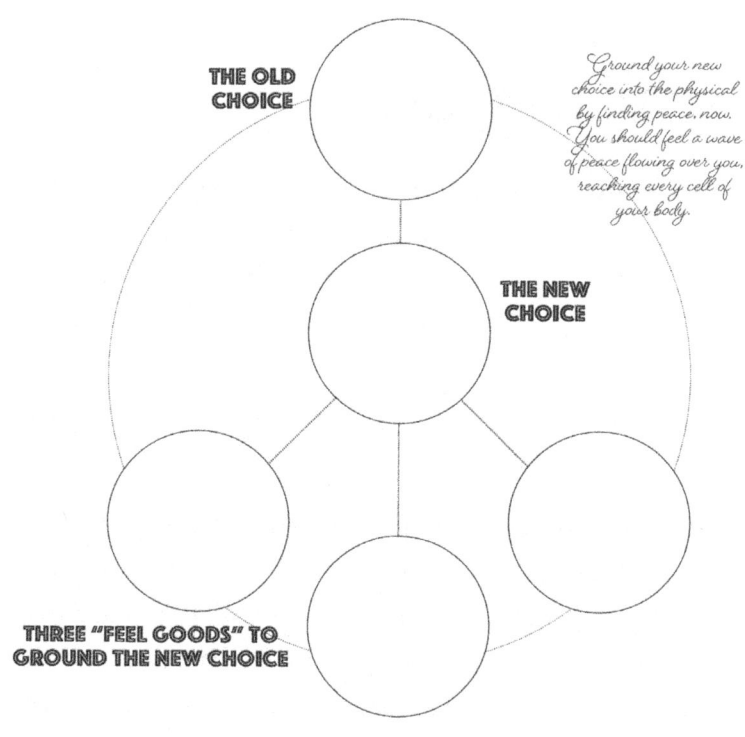

THE OLD CHOICE

Ground your new choice into the physical by finding peace, now. You should feel a wave of peace flowing over you, reaching every cell of your body.

THE NEW CHOICE

THREE "FEEL GOODS" TO GROUND THE NEW CHOICE

JOURNALING PROMPTS

- Is the 5U Healing Process helpful to you? Why or why not?

- Is the Reflection Journaling Practice helpful to you? Why or why not?

- How can you take what you've learned about healing in the last several chapters and combine it with your previous knowledge and your favorite healing modality?

FEELING STUCK?

- **Learn more about the Reflection Journaling Practice.** You can grab a printable of this practice to test it out, or I have several book versions of the practice if you'd like a smaller journal that you can carry with you on the go. http://cardreadingqueen.com/reflection-journaling-practice/

- **Download the 5U Healing Process Cheat Sheet.** You can post this on your wall or in your journal or planner so you have the process with you and easily accessible at all times. You can also grab my printable on turning the 5U process into your preferred healing modality, so that you can create a unique meditation, tarot spread, astrology reading, and more. Learn more about the 5U Healing Process here: http://cardreadingqueen.com/5u

- **Check out the Core Wound Wheel Cheat Sheet** which helps you identify and name the wounding you are experiencing now. This can be extremely helpful in the Upset Phase of the 5U Healing Process. Get the cheat sheet at http://cardreadingqueen.com/core-wound-wheel/

Chapter Twelve

SETTING BOUNDARIES ON THE TWIN SOUL JOURNEY

O ne of the darkest periods between my husband and me happened just two years after we got married. We had both experienced abusive relationships in the past and found ourselves dealing with toxic behavior in our marriage as well. We had some explosive fights that were rooted in control and dominance, and neither of us were fighting completely fairly.

As my husband talked about having children, I found myself taken back to my previous marriage where my ex-husband had also brought up the topic of kids. In that marriage, I had thought, "No way would I ever want to bring children into this relationship." In that marriage, I had dealt with slammed doors, thrown objects, name-calling, yelling, intense criticism and belittling, damage and attempted damage to my personal property, and my ex-husband being unkind to our pet dog. The realization that I didn't want to have children with my ex-husband, for the child's sake, was what finally helped me leave the marriage, as I couldn't seem to do it for myself or my own happiness and safety.

Although the toxicity in my new marriage wasn't nearly as bad as what I experienced before, I found myself having nearly the same reaction. "No way would I ever want to bring children into this relationship." And as I unpacked why, I found that at the core, I had zero tolerance for name-calling, abuse, belittling, or any sort of violent and uncontrolled physical behavior. As a child, I had never experienced this between my parents, and I realized that the only thing that had normalized it for me in my relationship with my husband was the fact that I had experienced it so much worse in my relationship with my ex-husband.

I laid out my terms to my husband: if we didn't end our patterns, I was leaving. At first, he thought that was ridiculous, saying that he couldn't control himself and that I just made him so angry. There was a lot of justifying, like, "if you didn't act like X, I wouldn't call you X." And then he questioned, "You're really going to leave me over a word?"

We attempted to bargain our way through this period. Could he go three months without saying X or doing Y? Was there any justification for certain behaviors? Why did he have to quit when I sometimes crossed the same lines I was drawing? And what if something slipped out? We bargained so much until I finally told him, "I believe you when you say you can't stop yourself, because you literally won't stop to save your marriage."

To no real surprise, bargaining didn't get us very far in solving the issue. This makes sense as bargaining is compromising and will never give two partners in a relationship deep fulfillment. It's just something society does to convince people to settle for less than what they want and deserve. And I did not want to settle as I had so many times before. I wanted to honor myself and my desire for zero tolerance around toxicity in my relationship.

We stewed in silence for months at this impasse. My husband would not agree to zero tolerance, because he didn't trust himself to be able to keep a promise like that. I would not agree to the relationship, because I didn't trust him to step up and respect me the way I wanted either. As we walked through this hallway, this transition between rooms, I used my healing practices to try to break through the block I was experiencing. I was 100% dead set on my boundary—I could feel that in my heart. But my husband was not reflecting that back to me. Did that mean he wasn't my twin soul? Did that mean we needed to part ways?

At some point in my healing work, something shifted for us. My husband told me that our relationship was the most important thing to him, and that the only reason he was calling me names was because he was projecting all of his own feelings about himself onto me.

I too, had an insight on my journey around the same time. I realized that my past trauma was keeping me from trusting that my husband could ever change his ways. I had never seen any past partner truly end their toxic behaviors. My ex-husband had only turned to manipulation and lies to hide his toxic behavior, from me as well as others around us. And I had easily fallen into labeling him a narcissist and sociopath to explain to myself why I couldn't make our relationship work.

I decided to release that narrative around both my ex-husband and my husband. *People are capable of change*, I told myself. With that new understanding, I found myself shifting in what I was trying to heal. Did I believe I could change? Did I believe that when I changed, my twin soul changed?

Not long after, my husband and I were able to resolve our problems. I was able to heal this for us spiritually and within myself, once I understood the intricacies of twin soul boundaries and how to set boundaries with your twin soul on this journey.

Boundaries are one of the most confusing parts of the twin soul journey. When I hear others talk about setting boundaries with their twin soul, they sound a lot like I did when I first approached my husband with my zero tolerance "boundary." I can tell you from personal experience, it doesn't work! But I know what does, and by the end of this chapter, you will understand too.

On the twin soul journey, there are truly only three entities you can set boundaries with—yourself, your twin soul, and your higher power. All other boundaries you set are just projections of one of these three beings.

If you cross a boundary with any of these three entities you'll usually get a slap on the wrist for trying to control things. This is not a big deal—use the 5U Healing Process or the Reflection Journaling Practice to heal it—but it is a little confusing when you first experience it and don't know what's happening. The problem is that the way society teaches healthy boundaries doesn't and can't work for a twin soul relationship. Healthy boundaries as society teaches them are ideal for temporary relationships, but impossible for relationships bound by the Twin Soul Trinity. In this chapter, we will discuss how to set boundaries with each entity in the Twin Soul Trinity.

SETTING BOUNDARIES WITH YOURSELF

There are many areas of your life where you are unlikely to have great boundaries. Again, don't stress about this—what you've been taught by society can't work for twin souls, because twin souls are meant to be in your life permanently, and the typical conversation around boundaries applies to temporary relationships. This is changing—society is evolving and you are part of bringing a new way to the collective consciousness. In the early and middle stages of your journey, though, this societal conditioning can easily trip you up with your twin soul.

Furthermore, the twin soul journey can make you feel a bit whacko at times. You are likely hyper-emotional because you have strong feelings for your counterpart. At the same time, you are getting hit with massive triggers no matter what the physical looks like. So how can you protect and respect yourself as you are going through an incredibly challenging ascension process?

Having boundaries with yourself around your twin soul work is truly the best way to keep yourself and your heart safe on this journey. Here are the boundaries I recommend for your twin soul journey:

#1 - MAKE YOURSELF YOUR TOP PRIORITY

Priorities are boundaries you set with yourself. Glennon Doyle writes in her book, *Untamed,*

> "I'll abandon everyone else's expectations of me before I'll abandon myself. I'll disappoint everyone else before I'll disappoint myself. I'll forsake all others before I'll forsake myself. Me and myself: We are till

|| death do us part."

You have to put you first on this journey, to the extent that you are not harming others, of course. This journey is one of uncovering all the places inside yourself that you've been compromising, hiding, running from, ignoring, avoiding, betraying, rejecting, shaming, blaming, and abandoning.

That doesn't mean that you ignore your twin soul, but it does mean that you will not have your twin soul until you are truly loving yourself as you are. You must be willing to see the truth of you to go deeper with your twin soul.

#2 - RESPECT SOMEONE'S STATED BOUNDARIES

Unrequited love is shamed in our society, but that's just another false belief. There is nothing less real about your love for someone just because it appears to not be returned in the physical. This journey is meant to show you that any relationship you have with anyone is only an inner experience. What you see on the outside is a reflection of your inner self and past choices you've made—not a reflection of the choices you are making now.

That said, if someone is stating that they have a boundary, it's important to honor that. It doesn't mean that you have to invest in the illusion, but you always have to accept what someone is showing you in the physical as that is where they are at with the process. Pushing your agenda because you "know the spiritual truth" of something is only the core wound of control. Your twin soul may be the same as you spiritually, but they will likely present themselves differently in the physical. Give them the space and love to explore and come to their own conclusions.

#3 - RESPECT SOMEONE'S PERSONAL SPACE

Not all boundaries are stated verbally but some are instead set by society. Your twin soul may be a spiritual connection, but they are also another person. You are not entitled to anything from your twin soul just because they are your twin soul. Your relationship may build slowly and naturally still, just as it would with any other person, even though you are twin souls. There is no need to physically force yourself on your twin soul. This includes touching them, but can also include forcing your presence on them, showing up uninvited, or touching their stuff.

#4 - RESPECT SOMEONE'S PHYSICAL RELATIONSHIP

The twin soul journey will never require you to interfere in someone else's relationship. You never need to break them up, to try to connect with them behind a partner's back, to cast a curse on their loved one, or to manifest their partner away. All of these things can only repel your twin by the Law of Attraction. Think about it:

- If you are your twin, and

- Your twin is attracted to something/someone, and

- You are repelled by or repelling that same something/someone, then

- You are also repelled by and repelling your twin!

This can be applied to anyone in their life and anything they are choosing.

Your twin soul is always trying to show you something, and you only ever need to do the healing work to unite with them. Anything you are doing to sabotage them in the 3D is not unconditional love, it's just the core wound of control.

Instead, make a new choice inside yourself and for yourself. If this is your twin they will make the same choice energetically. That choice may manifest differently in the physical in the short term, but if this is your true twin soul, they will eventually be attracted to you.

#5 - ASK FOR CONSENT

If you desire to send something to your twin:

- **Energetic love** - always okay

- **Energetic healing** - ask for energetic/soul consent

- **A message (via text, email, or social)** - okay as long as you are not blocked or crossing a stated boundary from the person

- **A physical message or gift** - Ask first and each time unless in a mutual relationship

- **A physical appearance** - Ask first and each time unless in a mutual relationship

Likewise, legal consent is necessary. Your twin-soul is not going to be an inappropriate age for you. You are not going to need to break any laws to connect with your twin. You are not going to need to do anything that would place you on a "suspect" list with authorities to get into your twin soul union.

#6 - FOLLOW YOUR OWN DISCERNMENT

The only way anyone can offer you advice is if they can trust you to not only make your own decisions, but take responsibility for your own decisions. It's a two-way street of trust. This is true for both general advice and one-on-one advice.

I have a deep compassion for those who do not have as much confidence, self-assuredness, and trust in their own decision-making. Often, there are events in one's life that caused this, and the good news is that it can be healed. I encourage my audience to heal this piece of the journey (connecting with and trusting their feelings, intuition, and internal logic systems) early on as discernment is an important part of the process.

As you consume my content, it's important to me that you take it only as it resonates for your situation and personality. I never claim to know anyone better than they know themselves, even in a one-on-one situation. Always trust your own decision-making and take responsibility for your decisions.

SETTING BOUNDARIES WITH YOUR TWIN SOUL

What about setting boundaries with your twin soul? I have had to do this many times on my journey, and I've made a number of mistakes that have repelled my twin soul from me! I did eventually figure out exactly what was happening and I will share with you the challenges that twin souls have with setting boundaries for each other on the journey.

#1 - SET BOUNDARIES, NOT ULTIMATUMS

The biggest mistake I see twin souls making is setting ultimatums rather than boundaries. This is a sneaky one because society praises those who create ultimatums in relationships! Furthermore, society mixes up ultimatums and boundaries and uses them interchangeably in most cases.

Remember, society has taught all of us that if someone isn't giving us what we want or meeting our needs, that we should discard them and move on to "someone who will treat us well." This sounds like good advice, but it doesn't work on the twin soul journey because you can't truly leave or move on from your twin soul. You can move on physically, but then you're just running. The only permanent solution when dealing with your twin soul is to work through things and end the toxic patterns of behavior.

Furthermore, on the twin soul journey, you are not trying to get what you want and need from an outside source like your romantic partner. That feels yucky and creates deep codependency. Instead, you are going to your true source, your higher power, and giving all of what you want and need to yourself first. Through doing this, your outer reality changes, and everything you're already giving to yourself shows up on the outside through your twin soul, your permanent partner and your higher power manifested as a person.

You cannot give your twin soul an ultimatum, because an ultimatum by definition is, "if you do/don't do X, I will do/don't do Y." This seems healthy, but it's actually a massive wounding around trying to control someone or control your journey. You are not meant to discard your twin soul and find someone else if they don't comply with your ultimatum. Thus, ultimatums don't work. In my experience, issuing ultimatums with your twin soul will only drive them away, and quickly, because they are designed to show you your deepest wounding.

So how do you get your twin soul to respect you and stop treating you like a doormat? The answer is to set a boundary. A boundary can only be set from a place of love. This is not something society teaches us to do.

STEP #1: HEAL THE UPSET COMPLETELY

Before you set a boundary, you first want to heal everything about what your twin soul is doing that is upsetting you. Use the 5U Healing Process and the Reflection Journaling Practice in the previous chapters to do this. This step is absolutely critical as you will not be able to set a boundary until you can come from a place of peace and love toward yourself and your twin soul.

STEP #2: CLEAN UP YOUR SIDE OF THE ROAD

Once you have healed yourself, you will naturally have a great deal more love, worthiness, and respect for yourself around the trigger. This is good. The next step is, whatever boundary you want to set with your twin soul, you must set and follow for yourself.

This likely doesn't apply to everyone, but it will apply to many if not most of those reading. For example, when my husband was in his name-calling phase, I desperately wanted him to stop... and at the same time I was a name-caller too!

I had my reasons. "He started it," or "he pushed me to do it." No, no, there are no excuses. Your twin soul will never honor a boundary that you yourself don't follow 100% every time, because they are you. They are merely showing you yourself by crossing your boundaries.

I sometimes hear examples like, "My twin soul cheated on me but I don't cheat on them." It's possible that you have nothing to clean up, but if this is your true twin soul, it's unlikely. Sometimes these boundaries manifest differently in the physical. Perhaps they cheated on you with another partner, but you cheated someone out of a ton of money. Use the healing tools to get really clear on where you might be crossing the same boundary energetically.

STEP #3: TELL THEM HOW TO CLEAN UP THEIR SIDE OF THE ROAD WITH LOVE

Now that you've healed your upset and gotten your own side of the road cleaned up and free of the toxic energy, it's time to communicate your boundary with your twin soul. You set a boundary from a place of loving the person no matter what, but outlining what you deserve from them, and knowing that if they are your true twin soul, you will receive your love from them.

To set a true boundary, you must be able to honestly express your unconditional love for the person and fully accept that you are 50/50 partners in this upset or trigger. A true boundary sounds like, "I love you, and you have to clean up your behavior around _____. This looks like…"

With true boundaries with your twin soul, there are no major consequences, no timelines, and no spoken or unspoken threats. It's a very different energy from an ultimatum because you are not intending to withdraw your love, regardless of what the person does. You are choosing to partner with your twin soul and take responsibility for healing the wound in your union. The person can still make their own choice, and you can love them through that choice by continuing to heal, detaching from outcome or any attempt to control your twin soul, and trusting that your twin soul will always return the love you give yourself.

What if you do all of this, you can feel deep in your heart that you are choosing love in this space, and your twin soul isn't returning the love that you give yourself? If this is the case, you have to discern whether you have more healing to do or whether this person is perhaps not your twin soul and instead a false or karmic twin. Your twin soul will always respond positively to clear and loving communication that comes from a place of deep peace.

In my experience from having a karmic twin, and then a twin soul, the difference was that my karmic twin didn't truly care about me or growing our love for each other in our relationship. He was willing to say or do anything that kept me around, even if it was lies or manipulation. My karmic twin did not care about partnership or solving the problems between us; he only cared about investing in more and more illusion.

With my twil soul, it was actually the opposite. He was honoring himself and what he needed, even if it wasn't what I wanted to hear. He was never trying to hurt me and only trying to heal our partnership. Your true twin soul cares about you, often beyond what they can express in words. They want to help you grow and they want to love you. The minute you do this for yourself, they are right there with you.

#2 - ERADICATE ADDICTIONS

Does your twin soul have addictive behaviors? Before I continue with this section, I want to encourage you to discern whether your twin soul's behavior is due to a physical addiction which requires professional intervention (please seek professional help for them as this is beyond the scope of this book), or if they have addictive tendencies or are using drugs, alcohol, or other substances to seek temporary highs or numb out.

My own story with addiction is that in my

mid-twenties, I drank about a bottle of wine by myself in an empty apartment, 3-4 nights a week, and spent the other nights going out and partying and drinking with friends. I had an abuse problem with alcohol that made me look like an alcoholic. The abuse did not begin overnight, but rather built from my late teens and early twenties when I partied a little too hard in college to avoid several challenges I was having with finding my divine purpose and my twin soul.

My wake up call happened when I had too much alcohol and not enough food (I frequently skipped meals in order to make room for drink calories during this period in my life) and crashed head first into a glass coffee table at a friend's apartment.

I walked away from that deeply embarrassed and realizing I needed to make changes in my life. Luckily, I did not have a physical addiction to alcohol and could easily abstain with no detoxification symptoms. In my observation, this is fairly common in twin soul relationships. If a person is truly addicted to substances, they are in such a vibration that would naturally repel their twin soul. I've seen that most twin souls who have found their way to the ascension journey and have some level of physicality to their union are rarely dealing with a full-blown addiction, and are instead dealing with substance abuse used to numb out to their wounds and upsets.

Once I realized I was not physically addicted, I was able to moderate my alcohol intake. I figured

SETTING BOUNDARIES ON THE TWIN SOUL JOURNEY

out that I was using alcohol to numb and escape, and as I healed my pain and wounding, I was able to completely release alcohol from my regular habits and stop drinking.

If your twin soul abuses substances or activities to distract themselves from pain, the mirror is usually around boundaries and more specifically, dependency and codependency. Addictions are a complete lack of boundaries around self and others. Your twin soul's addictive behaviors are likely a deep reflection of your own lack of boundaries in some area of your life. Use the healing tools shared in this book to release your own patterns around codependency and boundaries so your twin soul can release their need to numb out and chase false highs.

Once again, please use your discernment to identify if your twin soul needs professional help. The spiritual work is meant as a supplemental aid to any professional help required. Additionally, please do not stay in a toxic situation or environment, regardless of whether the person in question is your twin soul or not. Your healing efforts can only help your twin soul, so a person who is not responding to your inner work is likely a false or karmic twin.

SETTING BOUNDARIES WITH YOUR HIGHER POWER

One of the most interesting attempts at boundaries I've seen on the twin soul journey is people trying to set boundaries with their higher power. This can take the form of:

- Denouncing your higher power

- Deciding not to believe in twin souls

- Avoiding the healing work

- Trying to quit the twin soul journey

- ... And so much more.

In general, if you have resentment toward the twin soul journey in any way, you likely are trying to set "boundaries" with your higher power.

No surprise here—these are usually ultimatums as described in the previous section, except this time you are giving your higher power the ultimatum.

- "Why do I do the healing work and not see results in the physical?"

- "How is this even my twin soul if they won't talk to me?"

- "If God is so great, why is he torturing me with this journey?"

- "I'm done with this journey. I want off the drama rollercoaster."

- "They are with someone else—am I just making up this connection?"

- "I need another sign or I can't move forward."

Do you see the ultimatum—the "if my higher power does/doesn't do X I will/won't do Y"—in each of these statements? Again, there is no reason to feel shame or blame around these thoughts and feelings, because they are very human and bound to come up along your journey. They are coming up so you can work through them and heal them, and everyone on the journey has to go through this part.

When people struggle with this journey, want to get off the journey, or think the journey is harmful to them, it usually comes down to a few misconceptions about what the journey is:

#1 - THEY ARE FIXATED ON A SPECIFIC PERSON

The goal of twin soul work is not to get a random person of your choosing to be your boyfriend or girlfriend. I see a lot of people on this journey who care much more about getting a specific person than about getting their twin soul. But as this book demonstrates, the only thing twin soul work can get you is a closer relationship to your higher power, which reveals the truth of you to you, which attracts your true twin soul.

When you have a deeper recognition of yourself, then you can truly see who your twin soul is with a clear heart, no ego. This person may not be who you expect. Do you want your twin soul, your ideal romantic partner? Or do you think you know better than your higher power who and what will make you happy?

If you have a person in mind who you think is your twin soul, it's safe to use them as a mirror to heal from. But if you feel that you are fixating on a specific person, gently return your attention to yourself and step more into who you are. Let your reality fall away or build up around you as you continue to heal your core wounds and seek the truth of yourself.

You never have to fixate on anything outside of yourself to manifest it—that is trying to create transformation in your outer world rather than your inner world. The process of manifestation is and only ever has been healing the separation within you... not creating something outside of you. Fixation is counter-productive to manifestation.

#2 - THINGS DON'T GO THE WAY THEY EXPECTED

Anyone on the twin soul journey wants to get to a milestone that marks progress. Ideally, this endpoint is that they are in a physical relationship with the person they think is their twin soul.

And often, if they don't get that person in an expected time period, or in an expected way, they start to resent and blame the journey itself, then try to take control (which is a fear-based wounding) of the situation by either forcing themselves off the journey or using the journey to justify crazier and crazier actions toward their twin soul.

Both are the same thing, ultimately: an attempt to control themselves and what is truly in their hearts, and an attempt to go against what their higher power is creating for them.

A friend of mine once pointed out that heartbreak is the distance between what you expected and what actually happened. This rang true for me immediately.

But manifestation requires releasing expectation to outcome. So if you're feeling heartbreak, isn't that really just another block to the manifestation?

Now, it's important to feel what you feel, always. But when you are able to come back to a place of understanding of what this journey really is, the heartbreak is truly just pointing to some core wounding that can continue to be cleared using the same methods as any other wound clearing.

In other words, the pattern of heartbreak was already there within you, buried in your subconscious. That heartbreak pattern has been brought to the conscious through this person you believe is your twin soul... which is exactly how this journey is intended to work, of course!

Twin soul work is actually the relief to the heartbreak that already resides within you. Once the heartbreak is in your consciousness you can heal all the aspects of it so you no longer repeat the patterns. All other paths are just escape/avoidance. You'll attract the same person again who will show you the same wounding within.

However, if you go into twin soul work with only the desire to heal your separation from your creator and yourself, then your twin soul will be revealed to you and you will be united with them.

Twin soul work is only about asking yourself what and who is truly in your heart. It's about healing your ego until you can see your heart clearly.

#3 - THEY WANT TO END THE PAIN

So why do all this work on yourself if the person you think is your twin soul doesn't end up being so? Or you don't end up in physical union with your crush? Does it make sense to reveal old core wounding from childhood if it's only going to cause more pain and heartbreak?

First, remember that the pain and heartbreak were already there, you are just revealing it to yourself consciously through your twin soul situation. It's coming up for release so you don't have to drag it around through life and all of your relationships, romantic or not.

Next, understand that while the pain and heartbreak can be great, and sometimes overwhelming, denying what's in your heart is not a path to lasting change.

Again, the wounding you don't look at, that you bury in your subconscious, can only grow. You are investing a lot of subconscious energy in that wounding without even realizing it. The more you attempt to ignore that wounding, the more your higher power will keep showing you that wounding through contrast.

There are two ways your higher power alerts you to your subconscious wounding. You can bring it to the surface and clear it through active healing. Or you can experience it and play it out in real life through contrast.

Contrast is experiencing what you don't want in order to understand and align to what you do want. So by the Law of Attraction, for any heartbreak you decide not to heal, you will continue to attract the pattern until you heal it:

- The person who blocked you

- The person with someone else

- The person who just wants to be friends

- The person who doesn't even want to be friends

- The person who it's only ever going to be a situationship with

- The person from your past

- The person you broke a commitment to

- And so on...

In the internet age, there's a growing trend of ghosting, blocking, or otherwise cutting people off. While this is supposedly to set boundaries, it's often used as an avoidance tactic instead.

It's really easy to escape a relationship, but that doesn't mean you healed it. It's all just going to pop up again with the next person. You can escape the relationship, but you can't escape yourself.

Finally, decide to process the pain rather than letting it sit in your inbox, cluttering you up and stealing your focus and energy. I remember sitting with so much pain as I began the journey, but I know now from experience that the pain is finite. You will eventually run out, just like if you were to deal with your incoming mail or inbox every day, you would eventually get down to a small and manageable number of messages.

And when you heal yourself, you are basically guaranteed to attract your twin soul through the process.

#4 - THEY FEEL LIKE THEY ARE NEVER GOING TO GET THEIR TWIN SOUL

What about people who don't get their twin soul? You may look around at the twin flame/ twin soul community and notice, "there are a lot of people who still seem single and miserable."

It's very easy to get stuck on this journey by not doing the healing work. The twin flame community is made up with a lot of people who really just want the drama of trying to use spirituality to force a specific person into a relationship with them.

There is also a smaller portion of the twin flame community who are using and applying the concepts of the Universal Laws and the Twin Soul Trinity to do their healing work, who simply don't have results in the physical yet. Their results are coming!

You can only not get your twin soul by not doing the work. If you are truly healing, then your true twin soul is on their way to you. If you heal and heal and the person you think is your twin soul is only moving further and further away from you, then they might not be your twin soul—and that's okay. Do you want your twin soul, your ultimate and permanent lover created by your higher power and designed to be with you? Or do you want a random person that you are in a relationship with out of your mutual wounding patterns? Release expectations around your twin soul, and they will come to you. This journey doesn't end when you reveal a false twin, because this journey is not about getting a specific person. It's about getting the truth and finding deep peace with who you really are and who your twin soul really is. This requires you to surrender your control over the process, to have faith, and to do your healing work.

#6—THEY FEEL LIKE IT'S ALL MADE UP

What if it's all made up? What if life really is random and chaotic? What if you don't truly have any cosmic connections with anyone, and we are all just little sticks of flesh and meat, pretending we mean something to someone?

I went through a period of believing in, "life sucks and then you die." What I eventually found was that it really doesn't matter if I believe in something bigger than me and it doesn't turn out to be true. This is partially because I'm not attached to my beliefs and I am open to the truth, whatever that may be.

But it's also because it truly doesn't matter. The only thing that matters is the present and finding ways to feel good in the present. This is done through telling better stories about your past. It is actually safe to tell yourself stories about your past, even if they are fiction or not rooted in "reality." People who do this are happier and more at peace. The story is what feels good.

If someone finds love and happiness, it doesn't matter if they think they found it through randomness or through a magical occurrence of signs, synchronicities, and destiny. So you get to choose—do you wish to believe in randomness, coincidence, and the disempowering system of distorted order and chaos? Or do you choose to believe in a magical, abundant, loving, peaceful, and joyful life for yourself? When in doubt, choose the best story you can come up with.

If you are unsure what you prefer, you can test both. The best way to understand your higher power is to go all-in and do what they are telling you to do. You can then see how your life compares to your old ways of doing things.

#7 - THEY DON'T WANT TO PARTNER WITH THEIR TWIN SOUL

The twin soul journey means that every energy your twin soul expresses is also within yourself somewhere. Lots of people want their twin soul to be a mirror when it's convenient rather than when they are truly in the deep end of healing core wounding with them. That's simply not what your higher power asks of you, nor is it was they promise to you. Every piece of your twin soul's energy is a reflection of your energy, and the sooner you truly accept that, the sooner you can be with your twin soul—without having it be trigger central day in and day out.

Your higher power is not going to support you and your twin soul in the physical until you get on board with this, as the two of you would only expand the bad feelings you're already experiencing.

But what if my twin soul is doing X? While you can't control your true twin soul on the outside, you can completely control your own energy. Shift your energy first through doing your healing work all the way to the core and to the best of your ability. Then look at what's being reflected to you with non-attachment. If this is your true twin soul, they will always reflect your healing back to you.

You can try to go half-in on the twin soul journey, but it's really going half-in on your higher power. Your higher power is only going to keep redirecting you to your wounding through your physical reality. When I tried to control Patrick through my external reality, he continued to defy me. It was only when I truly did the healing work and transformed my energy, solely for myself, that he did the same. He did not do it for me; he did it because he no longer wanted to experience toxicity in his reality. Your twin soul is never going to do the thing before you do the thing. They are not going to go first; you will take the exact same energetic step at the same time. That is the true power of this journey.

JOURNALING PROMPTS

- Where do you feel you struggle to set boundaries with or prioritize yourself? What support can you give yourself in this?

- Where do you struggle with toxic or controlling behavior toward others? Where can you set a boundary for yourself around your behavior?

- When have you set boundaries that have

worked? When have you thought you were setting a boundary but you were really giving your twin soul or romantic partner an ultimatum? How did these situations turn out?

- Where do you find yourself doubting your higher power or the twin soul journey? Is there an ultimatum in your doubts?

FEELING STUCK?

- **Release attachment to your twin soul.** If you are struggling specifically with trying to set boundaries for yourself or with your higher power on the twin soul journey, I encourage you to check out my book, *Breaking the Twin Soul Connection: Safely Ending the Pain, Intensity, Heartbreak, Obsession, Depression, and Feeling of Dying That You May Be Experiencing On Your Journey (Twin Soul Hearts in Union #6)*. This book can help you work through the rollercoaster of emotions—obsession, intensity, depression, unrequited love, and more—and step instead into peace and surrender to the process. This is not a bait and switch—you really can release your attachment to the person you think is your twin soul, so that you can free up the energy of your twin soul journey and move it forward. Learn more about the book here: http://cardreadingqueen.com/books/

- **Get the Twin Soul Encouragement Deck.** It's not easy to do the healing work—I get it! I have been in resistance to healing work in the past, questioning whether it was easier to numb out instead of investing more deeply. This deck lovingly shares messages that will gently tune you to the twin soul vibration. You can pull cards virtually from all of my decks for free, or you can learn more about a physical copy of the deck at http://twinsouloracle.com

Chapter Thirteen
TWIN SOUL MYTHS AND COMMON QUESTIONS

I started this journey back in 2017 to better understand my relationships, but I found so much more as I dived deeper into the twin soul literature that I could find online and combined it with my own experiences and ideas. In this chapter, I want to rapid-fire answer a number of common questions in the twin soul community. Everything I have shared so far in this book about this journey is more than enough to get you started on chipping away at your particular cocktail of wounding and healing. At the same time, it can be helpful to see the previous chapters in action when it comes to a specific challenge or situation you are facing.

I've grouped these common twin soul questions into several sections:

- Uniting or Reuniting With Your Twin Soul

- Twin Soul Communication Blocks
- The Masculine and Feminine Dynamic
- Twin Soul Telepathy
- Other Common Major Upsets on the Journey

Each of these sections needs its own book or resource to explore deeper, so I've included links to resources that may be of assistance to you if you are dealing with a specific problem.

Additionally, I also recommend searching my Card Reading Queen website and blog, my Monica Grace Youtube channel, and my Your Twin Soul Journey podcast as I have answered over 100 questions about the twin soul journey for free through these mediums. It's possible that I've done an episode on many aspects of your specific journey and situation!

UNITING OR REUNITING WITH YOUR TWIN SOUL

ARE TWIN SOULS MEANT TO REUNITE IN THIS LIFETIME?

Twin souls are always united spiritually, but reunite in the physical when they've healed the separation between themselves and their romantic love from their higher power.

WHY SHOULD I REUNITE WITH MY TWIN SOUL?

The first and foremost reason is because you desire to be with your twin soul and receive your romantic love from them.

Additionally, your higher power supports your union because the two of you are masculine and feminine, and the more you connect, the more you are able to create in the world. You may be interacting energetically at the spiritual level, and maybe even at the emotional and/or mental levels, but coming together physically will turn up the dial on your interactions.

Because when you come together, you create more, you will only come together with your twin soul when you are going to create more love (and expand and grow in your higher power's mission) instead of creating more conflict, fear, and contrast.

IS MY TWIN SOUL ON THE OTHER SIDE?

It's possible but unlikely, as the two of you make the same energetic choices. If you are here on earth, then it would be difficult for them to make a vastly different core choice to not be on earth. Twin souls do descend on earth and leave earth at different times, but the high end of the age gap is typically not more than twenty years, with the majority of twin souls coming to earth within a few years of each other.

DOES MY TWIN SOUL OR DO I NEED TO GO THROUGH A KARMIC TWIN, FALSE TWIN, OR SOULMATE BEFORE WE UNITE?

There's no reason to go through other relationships to unite with your twin soul. Many people do because they find the twin soul journey later in life, after they've already had one or more serious relationships. If you were to learn about twin souls and do the inner work as a teenager, you could unite with your twin soul on the first try. If you choose to be single now, do the inner work, and release your attachment to any person being your twin soul, you could find your twin soul on the first try as well. It doesn't matter how many partners you go through to get to your twin soul, so don't worry if you are experiencing a relationship with someone who is not your twin soul right now.

WOULDN'T I BE HAPPIER WITH A SOULMATE THAN MY TWIN SOUL?

This question is founded in a belief that the twin

soul connection is difficult and painful. The twin soul journey is actually what helps you get rid of the pain. It's the solution rather than the problem. To get rid of the pain, you do have to feel and heal the pain first, but even that feels good when you accept and understand the process.

If you desire to ascend, you will be happier uniting with your twin soul. Your twin soul is your partner in ascension, so to be with a soulmate would mean not partnering on ascension.

ARE DARK FORCES KEEPING ME FROM MY TWIN?

No, dark forces are an illusion. Dark forces are just the absence of light forces, the same way that the Devil is the absence of God and that separation is the absence of union.

To recognize dark forces as a separate entity would mean that they are of equal and opposite power to light forces. In truth, dark forces are nothing. They are an illusion, and simply a point on the spectrum of light forces. For more about this, see Chapter 7 on the Law of Polarity.

SHOULD I DATE OTHERS WHILE HEALING WITH MY TWIN?

There's no harm in dating others while you are healing, but be sure you are guided to them for the right reasons.

Are you dating because you have genuine interest in these potential partners and are being led by your heart? Are you actively doing your healing work, growing closer to your higher power, and following your higher power's guidance to co-create a beautiful life for yourself?

Or are you dating to make your twin soul jealous, to manipulate your twin, to indulge in carnal pleasure, or to cope with and numb out to the pain of loneliness, boredom, and other negative feelings?

If you are coming to dating because you are guided by your heart and soul, you can feel free to date as it will likely provide additional healing or clear additional karma. If you are coming to dating to avoid your healing and self-medicate, it may make more sense to opt out of the dating scene.

HOW DO I UNITE OR REUNITE WITH MY TWIN SOUL IN THE PHYSICAL?

I sense there is a desire for an exciting answer here, but the truth is that your healing work will unite you with your twin soul in the physical. Study the twin soul work and keep choosing to create true and permanent peace in all areas of your life; all the love you desire will easily follow.

WHAT DO YOU DO WITH YOUR TWIN SOUL WHEN YOU UNITE OR REUNITE WITH THEM?

Your main purpose for uniting with your twin soul is for romance, love, and fulfillment in your personal life. From there, the two of you will work on your divine purpose, home, health, and wealth together. Allow these partnerships in each of these areas to unfold naturally and in the perfect order and timing.

HOW DO YOU LEARN YOUR DIVINE PURPOSE WITH YOUR TWIN SOUL?

The best way to learn your purpose with your twin soul is to unite with your twin in the physical, as this level of interaction will spark the most outward creation for you and your partnership.

If you are not united with your twin, you are safe to explore your purpose on your own. It will likely lead you to your twin. The minute I committed to my true life purpose (after years of denying myself and it) I also started a relationship with my twin soul, though I didn't know it was him at the time. Your divine purpose is a natural catalyst for your true twin soul to join you in life.

You can further explore your purpose through astrological natal charting and synastry, tarot readings, and communication with your higher power. If you would like a reading from me, please contact team@cardreadingqueen.com for my current offerings.

TWIN SOUL COMMUNICATION BLOCKS

WHY DID MY TWIN SOUL BLOCK ME?

In talking to both twins who have blocked each other and twins who have been blocked, the experience is deeply painful on both ends. There are a few reasons that one twin blocks the other:

- **Violation of set or unspoken boundaries, often around communication -** If your twin asks you to stop texting or messaging him/her, and you choose not to, the connection can get blocked to protect the union. Violating boundaries is one thing that causes breaks between people, so the universe will never let you push your twin to the point of no return. This is also for your benefit, so you can banish codependent feelings like addiction, uncommunicated and unmet expectations, abandonment, betrayal, and more.

- **Inability to handle the pain of communicating with the other -** Sometimes there is a lot of pain associated with the relationship, especially if you have history with your twin soul. When people operate from a place of pain, they can truly hurt one another and say things they don't mean that destroy their connection. The universe will do whatever is necessary to protect the connection, thus may provide distance in communication until the two counterparts are able to reconnect from a place of love.

- **Running from the union, usually trying to cut the other person out of their life using typical 3D methods** - Many twin soul counterparts try at least once and often many times to completely cut a person from their life using traditional 3D methods. These are often ones that are featured in issues of *Cosmo* under articles labeled, "How to Get Over Your Ex FAST." I myself had tried to do this countless times with my twin soul until I finally found a way to do the healing work. Try not to take it personally if you sense your twin is doing this to you. This connection feels so challenging and painful at times, and it's human nature to want to end that pain in any way possible. Please know that if you are true twins, this effort on your twin's part will not work. They will always come back. They can't let you go any more than you can let them go.

- **Integration of closeness and healing -** Sometimes the two counterparts are in close contact and then one blocks the other. This can feel like it's coming out of nowhere, but ultimately it's the universe creating distance where there was once closeness so the two counterparts can integrate the healing they've received from each other (through triggering, through conversations, or more).

WHY WON'T MY TWIN SOUL RESPOND TO MY MESSAGES?

Often, a twin soul will not block communication, but will be slow to return messages or will opt not to respond at all. Sometimes, they will respond to some messages but not others. Sometimes, they will respond only if you pester them several times.

Many of the reasons that a twin soul blocks the other still apply. In this case though, the twin soul who is not responding acknowledges, sometimes only subconsciously, that they don't want to cut off the connection completely. They may have even considered blocking you, but something is keeping them from pulling the trigger.

This is a good sign because it shows that even if your messages are annoying them, there is some part of their soul that understands that they cannot run away from you.

There are some additional things that may be going on in this instance:

- **They have disinterest in the 3D -** Sometimes the universe distracts one twin or the other (at different times, even) so that the connection doesn't move forward as quickly for whatever reason. This can also be about protection of the union, as the universe will always protect the union from over-triggering that may cause the two to go in their separate directions. One twin may be directed to invest energy elsewhere to keep the two from interacting as much.

- **They are overwhelmed by Tower Moments -** If you are a divine feminine and have been actively healing your wounds, you may be experiencing your divine masculine going through Tower Moment after Tower Moment and feeling completely overwhelmed as his world falls apart. Have empathy for this as it's challenging to ground all that energy into the 3D. Remember that Tower Moments can be both positive and negative, from a job promotion to a move to a new relationship, and from a car accident to a health issue to a sick toddler to a family fall out.

- **They are sorting out their feelings for you -** One or both twins may have complicated and confusing feelings that he/she hasn't sorted those out yet. These feelings can range from hatred to annoyance to acceptance to frustration to romance to love. Many people are not equipped with ways to sort their feelings, and many will be cautious to communicate until they find clarity about how they feel and what they want from you.

- **There are topics that they are not ready to discuss with you -** If you are getting a hot/cold vibe from their messaging (e.g. they message back immediately sometimes and don't message back at all other times), pay attention to the questions or topics you are asking them. There may be topics or questions that don't capture their interest, or that you are not meant to know their thoughts on yet. They may have nothing particular to say about it at that moment, so it washes over them Westworld-style.

- **They are conserving energy -** Healing is a lot of work, and depending on what else is happening in their lives, they may have responsibilities to attend to or dreams and goals to work out solutions for. They can't always pursue the connection at the same time as you.

IF THIS IS MY TWIN SOUL, WHY WON'T THEY CONTACT ME?

You have your twin on your mind all the time, so why doesn't he/she have you on the brain too? This is one of the most confusing challenges of a no/low contact separation period. You are always the one to initiate conversation (they rarely contact you un-prompted), and when you do, they don't always re-spond.

The obvious, 3D answer is that they are not in-terested in talking to you. You can take that answer further and believe they are too nice (or immature) to simply give you a direct, "I'm not interested" mes-sage. If it's a twin soul, however, it's truly not that simple!

If you'd like to know why they are not contacting you, read over the nine reasons I've already given in this section (under "Why did my twin soul block me?" and "Why won't my twin soul respond to my messag-es?") and see if any of them resonate with you. You can feel it in your heart if one of them is more rele-vant to your situation than others. This 3D explana-tion can sometimes be helpful to you to create peace where you didn't have it before, but I encourage you to use the healing process in tandem to choose your full peace around this now.

If none of these reasons resonate, then look inside and ask yourself, "What is coming up for me? How is this making me feel? Where am I being triggered?"

Make a list. You can use the Reflection Journaling Practice to work through each of these wounds systematically.

When you have healed your wounding around this, try again to see if anything resonates. You may also allow your intuition to drift to the answer. Trust whatever comes up for you, as you are connected to your twin soul at all times and have a direct line to their thoughts and feelings. All you have to do is tap into it!

HOW CAN I MANIFEST CONTACT FROM MY TWIN SOUL?

Would you like to receive contact from your twin soul? This is an easy 4-step process.

STEP 1: SHIFT YOUR EMOTIONS

Many people think that manifestation starts with your thoughts, but in my experience it starts with your emotions. Your emotions are where much of your wounding, triggering, blockage, and self-sabotages come from.

Shifting your emotions is simply about coming to peace with your situation. Simple, of course, but not easy! Allow yourself time with this.

A few things you can do (I recommend all three!):

- Ask yourself, "What is coming up for me? How is this making me feel? Where am I being triggered?" Make a list. You can use the Reflection Journaling Practice to work through each of these wounds systematically.

- Create an affirmation. Every morning (and throughout the day if you'd like), say out loud to yourself, "I love my twin. I welcome their communication style and whatever makes them comfortable. They deserve all the time in the world to message me back." Feel free to put your own spin on this! As you speak this out loud, notice where this affirmation is triggering you. You can feel the emotions stirring up in your body, and you can hear your mind contradicting the statement.

- Perform a simple ritual. Get some rose quartz (love) and lapis lazuli (communication/throat chakra) and put them in a small pouch or satchel that you can keep at your bedside or under your pillow. Allow these crystals to charge with your emotions around this situation while you sleep. When you wake up, run these crystals under some water and let the water carry away these emotions, down the drain of your sink. You can take these crystals to your bath, too!

Do each of these efforts, daily if possible, until you can feel the peace around this situation in your heart. When your emotions are at peace and you have reached a place of unconditional love and empathy for your twin, you are ready to manifest!

STEP 2: DECIDE WHAT YOU WANT

This step is easy! All you have to do is decide the communication you want to receive. Who do you want communication with? When do you want the communication to come? What method do you want the communication in (a call, text, conversation)? What do you want the content of the communication to be? Do you want this prompted or unprompted?

Where are you standing, sitting, etc. when you receive this communication? What are you wearing? How is the light pouring into the room? What mood are you in?

Write all of this out in detail, including your emotions. How do you feel when you receive this communication? What do you follow up with? Where does it lead to?

You are creating a textual vision board of an exact moment. DETAIL is important! Write it out!

Now, let's do a reality check. As you read over your vision, is anything in it a complete fantasy? For example, do you want someone to text you when they don't have your number? Do you want someone to show up at your door when they live in another state? Do you want someone to declare their love for you when you've seen no 3D signs of interest?

Your vision has to feel like it could really happen to you. It can't feel like a movie, a fairytale, or someone else's lucky life. The scene needs to play out in complete peace. Revise as necessary until every element of the vision is real and is something you believe could easily happen between you and your twin soul.

If you're feeling deflated regarding this, think of the smallest communication step your union can take and manifest that. Remember that you can use this process again once the first step has been completed!

STEP 3: TAKE ACTION

Now that you have a solid vision, you have to take action to make it real:

- If there's anything in your vision that you can do, take action on it. It could be sending communication. It could be spending time in the room from your vision and daydreaming about receiving that text. It could be communicating your vision to your best friends (who are cheering on your efforts).

- Choose colors and music for your vision. What is the perfect soundtrack, the perfect lighting, the perfect outfit, the perfect set, the perfect imagery? Make it feel real and bring your emotions around this vision to life!

Now, when you hear this song, or enter this room, or wear these colors, you'll automatically be reminded of the feel-good emotions of this beautiful communication you are going to receive.

- Reload your vision into your mind whenever it feels good (and only if it feels good). You may want to at least do this morning and evening. It's very important not to force it though. Do it for fun, but don't do it because you are afraid it won't happen if you don't do it (that's just inviting fear into your vision)!

- Choose a method of communication with your spirit team and the universe. You need a symbol for this communication. Pick anything of significance that you want: a number sequence, a spirit animal, a favorite image, a phrase—whatever you want! Whenever you see this symbol, it's a little reminder from the universe that they've received your vision and they are working to bring it toward you.

STEP 4: RECEIVE

The last step of any manifestation is to receive! This sounds like sitting back and sipping tea while your communication moves toward you, but there's actually a little more to it than that.

To start, you must release your vision from your emotions and thoughts.

Let me explain. Your vision is like an order you placed at a restaurant. Let's say you want spaghetti with meatballs and meat sauce, with a side salad that has no tomatoes (not even those cherry ones) and Italian dressing. Also, chopsticks, because that's how you like to eat spaghetti. And could they please bring out salad first, with one of those huge black pepper grinders because you like salad freshly peppered?

(Now if you're reading that and thinking, "what a high-maintenance order," go right back to Step 1 and start the whole process again!)

When you place an order like this, there's a lot that can go wrong, right? Especially if you can't see your waiter (the universe) writing anything down. Eek.

How do you spend the next 20 minutes while your food is being prepared? Do you sit there anxiously, wondering if they are going to forget about the no tomatoes part? Do you worry that the order never got placed and everyone else at the table will get their food before you? Do you look at your watch every few seconds to make sure your order is on track? Do you ask your waiter every time he walks by, "hey, is my order still coming?" Do you spend your time talking about the order, thinking about the order, hoping and wishing the order will come sooner?

No, of course not.

Instead, you have a glass of wine, you eye flirt with your partner, you tell stories to your friends, you laugh, and you appreciate all the beauty that surrounds you!

Once you've placed the order, release it and trust that the universe is bringing it to you.

Now let me explain what seems like a conflict, because I've also told you in step 3 to reload your vision.

While you're waiting for your food, you sometimes have moments of anticipation. "Mmm... I can't wait to try my spaghetti! Yum." These thoughts float in your mind and your emotions, getting you excited for what's coming. You may be experiencing smells or visuals (other people receiving their food) that remind you of your upcoming experience.

In fact, in the restaurant, you are automatically in a super high-vibe environment that is attuned to receiving beautiful food orders from your waiter. That's a big reason why you don't worry about the order that you placed. There are dozens if not hundreds of sensory cues that you are going to receive exactly what you asked for.

The same is true for your vision! In Step 2, you placed your order. In Step 3, we set up a high-vibe environment that is constantly winking at you to show you that your order is coming.

As you are waiting for your communication, lean into the high vibes of your environment and enjoy a little buzz of satisfaction every time you see hints of your vision coming toward you.

And while you are doing so, enjoy the beauty

and company that surrounds you. This is part of the high-vibe environment as well, and your positivity and happiness is exactly what creates your manifestation in your 3D reality.

So release that vision, sink into the beauty of the environment you've created for your vision to manifest, and enjoy exactly how the vision is unfolding in the meantime. This the energy of receiving. Feel it, know it, love it. Life is bliss!

WHY DOES MY TWIN SOUL SEND MIXED SIGNALS?

This is a challenging situation to experience, as it feels like your twin soul is just yanking your chain or toying with you. In truth, they are in a deep amount of inner pain and turmoil that is causing them to say one thing, do another, say another, feel another. There are a few possibilities:

- **They are healing the blocks that are keeping you both apart** - Your twin may think, say, and even feel like they are not interested in you, while part of them subconsciously gravitates toward you still. They may be more interested in being friends, or they may feel like they can't offer more at this time. This is a good thing, because your twin is putting the brakes on the connection and trusting their instincts about what is still needed to heal.

Look at where they pull back and ask yourself why. What is the block that they are healing, and what is the block that you are healing?

- **They are confused about their feelings for you** - I'm an avid fan of young adult novels and more specifically, love triangles, often portrayed as one girl who has the attention of two boys. Usually, the girl is confused about her feelings for each of her choices, as each person meets a different set of her needs. She experiments and tests, having moments with both boys, to better understand herself and what she needs. On the outside, it looks like she's playing both, but in reality she isn't. This is what your twin soul is doing too! There may not even be another person, but instead another dream, goal, belief, or way of life. He or she is testing both realities and learning more about him/herself in the process. Through experiencing many options, he/she clears and heals what's keeping them away from choosing a reality with you.

- **You are triggering them and they pull away as a result** - Closeness between you will cause triggers, which then causes both you and your twin to pull away. Perhaps they flirt with you one day, then the next say they shouldn't have or otherwise pull back. While this is incredibly hurtful, please understand that the connection between the two of you is like a teeter totter, rocking back and forth, first in huge movements, then in smaller ones as it comes to equilibrium. You may be in the "huge movements" phase right now, but trust that the dissonance will get smaller and smaller until you are both in perfect harmony, on the same exact wavelength.

HOW CAN I TELL MY PARTNER ABOUT TWIN SOULS?

There are many ways to tell your partner about twin souls, but before you do, you first must release all control, expectations, and attachments. Your twin soul may be your person but that doesn't mean the two of you will agree on everything on the surface. In spiritual truth you are never in disagreement; in physical truth, you may appear to be in disagreement as this is what you are meant to heal. As a result, sometimes twins come from different countries, different religions, different political parties, and more. You are meant to heal this and see that there is no separation between these different affiliations and belief systems.

When you have truly healed and released all control, expectations, and attachments around how they might react, how they might agree or disagree, and how they might take the news, you can try a few options:

- **Send them my book.** No seriously, you can! People share books with the people they love all the time. Tell them you have been reading and interesting book and you'd like to share a copy with them.

- **Watch a twin flame or twin soul video** online when they are in the room or when you are sitting next to them. See if their ears perk up.

- **Tell them that you have been studying a concept called twin souls.** They'll likely say, "I've heard about that," or "Twin souls—what is that?" Now you can have a conversation with them about it.

- **Ask them if they ever experience signs and synchronicities** and what they think it means when they see X or Y. This opens the opportunity for you to talk about the signs you're seeing and what they might mean for the relationship.

- **Tell them that you feel the relationship is special in some way,** and ask them if they have noticed anything. Describe twin souls without giving it a label. See if the descriptions resonate with them.

You'll see that once you've released your expectations around what others think of twin souls, it's actually quite easy to talk about twin souls.

There are a few other blocks to this one that I want to address:

1. **Twin souls are not a weird thing.** The concept is embedded into all the greatest love stories we tell, all the music we write, and all of our desires for our lives that we become aware of at a very young age. Because you are one consciousness, your true twin soul is as awakened as you are to the feelings and emotions behind twin souls, even if they don't have the words.

2. **You never need to prove the truth of twin souls to your twin or to anyone else.** Truth doesn't need to be proven, and people come into the truth of things in their own time. When my husband and I were struggling to manifest our child, I frequently asked him, "if we already knew our child and they told us they need more time before they can be born into this world, wouldn't we desire to grant them that?" As a parent, I would give my child all the time in the world to be ready to come to Earth. The same can be true for your twin soul. Unconditional love means releasing your time table and allowing them theirs.

THE MASCULINE AND FEMININE DYNAMIC

AM I THE MASCULINE OR THE FEMININE IN THE UNION?

The simplest way to figure out if you're the masculine or feminine in your union is to ask yourself which of these energies you truly would prefer:

- **Divine Masculine** – Responsible, Vulnerable, Adventurous, Courageous, Solutions-Oriented, Logical, Pursuant, Protective, Grounded, Giving, Providing, Action-Oriented, Leading, Boundary Setter, Steadfast

- **Divine Feminine** – Magnetizing, Expressive, Flowing, Self-Assured, Manifesting, Intuitive, Creative, Developing, Educating, Centered, Receiving, Nurturing, Connective, Collaborative, Candid, Faithful

Try each set of energies on for size. Which one feels peaceful to you? This is the one that you are.

You can also watch my content, How to Tell If You're the Masculine or Feminine Twin Soul: https://cardreadingqueen.com/masculine-or-feminine-twin-soul/

WHY DOES IT SEEM LIKE MOST MASCULINES ARE UNAWAKENED AND MOST FEMININES ARE CHASING THEM?

As twins awaken, the masculine focuses more on self on the journey, while the feminine focuses more on union. There is an illusion here as the self and the union are actually the same thing because of the Twin Soul Trinity, so the two counterparts are truly on two seemingly different roads that lead to the same destination.

In the physical, however, it can look to the feminine like she is the "awakened" one and her masculine is suddenly extremely selfish and ignoring her. This is a big part of the healing process that everyone must go through on the journey. If you are experiencing this, heal whatever is coming up for you as that is the only way through it!

WHY AM I DOING THE HEALING FOR BOTH OF US?

This question is most often asked by divine feminines and requires some explaining about how the twin soul connection works.

The divine feminine is in many ways, the dreamer or manifestor of the relationship in the 3D. The counterparts choose the relationship together in the 5D, but the divine feminine can often articulate to herself and verbally out loud what's going on long before the divine masculine can.

As the divine feminine does the healing through receiving and self-care modes, like meditation, journaling, rituals, tarot and oracle, crystals and essential oils, moon bathing, and so much more, the divine masculine will ground the healing into the 3D through taking action in his own life. What he thought he knew and believed no longer works for him anymore, and he has to release it. It was never built on a true foundation, just the illusion of one.

WHY DO BAD THINGS HAPPEN WHEN I DO MY HEALING WORK AND ESPECIALLY WHEN I'VE HEALED SOMETHING BIG WITH MY COUNTERPART?

I've seen versions of this question from the feminine who is doing the active healing work and then sees her masculine do something big, like ghost her, date someone new, move to another city, get engaged, get married, or have a child with someone else. This can be extremely frustrating to the feminine. So let's break down what's really happening.

First, the twin soul journey does not make "bad things" happen. Challenges are a part of life and the twin soul journey does not offer a life free of challenge—that is just ego and control that desires that. You cannot manifest away all bad, disappointing, or painful things in your life by "playing by the rules." Many feminines get stuck in this "good girl" trap which is really just control wounding that keeps you numbed out.

Instead, the twin soul journey makes any bad feelings you have about the situations and circumstances that come up in your life mundane. The goal of the twin soul journey is that you feel safe to feel your feelings at all times because bad feelings cannot harm you or take away your peace. You will still experience bad feelings, but you can handle them because you have the healing tools to do so. This makes the bad feelings as mundane as needing to refill your gas tank on your vehicle. It's a minor annoyance, but there is a gas station just down the block. It'll just take a minute to fix.

When you feel your feelings, you get to be present with life. You create a state of peace where you genuinely feel good most of the time. Anytime you feel bad, you can heal it and come back to a place of peace easily. This is what attracts your twin soul.

WHAT IS BLOCKING MY TWIN SOUL FROM ACKNOWLEDGING OUR CONNECTION?

The twin soul connection can be challenging to acknowledge and understand. There are so many things that a person must believe to truly acknowledge the twin soul connection:

- **You must believe in "The One"** - The belief in "The One" or your "person" is the belief that love is not random and that the ideal partner is not substitutable or replaceable. Believing that two hearts are destined to be together, but just need to find each other, is the gateway to entering the twin soul journey and your larger spiritual awakening toward ascension.

- **You must believe in a higher power** - While that belief may come in the form of believing in God, the Universe, Spirit, Source, or another creator, this is a tall order for many people, especially those formerly scarred by religion. In other words, you must have found a sense of spirituality, or a personal connection to a higher power, to believe in twin souls. Twin souls are ultimately based on the belief that as you grow closer to your higher power, you also grow closer to your greatest love in the 3D.

- **You must believe in the Universal Laws** - The Twin Soul Trinity is built on New Thought/ New Age principles around the Universal Laws, as well as the concept of divine order. It takes time to study this way of thinking and time to test it for yourself in the real world.

- **You must believe that this connection is THE connection** - Even if your twin soul believes in twin souls, does he/she see that *you* are the twin soul they've been searching for?

- **You must believe that this is a journey above all** - Your twin soul may do all sorts of things in the material world that don't align to what you want from them. This is a journey of healing for you, and as you heal, they heal. The surface of this connection—what they say, how they feel, what they think, what they do, who they spend time with, what they want— is all an illusion. If they are mired in separation consciousness, they are going to struggle to see through that illusion. You can use the healing tools in this book on this block and move through it if you are experiencing this from your twin soul.

You can use this list as a starter for diagnosing why your twin soul won't acknowledge your connection. Do you find yourself tripping up on any of these points? Do you know for a fact that your twin soul is tripping up on these points? This may be what's happening!

The best way to move your twin soul toward acknowledging the connection is to discuss these high-level concepts with your twin, not necessarily in the context of how they apply to your union. Get their thoughts on these concepts and share your own thoughts in a non-attached way.

This is also why I recommend sending them *Your Twin Soul Journey*, as it goes through each of these beliefs in great detail. It's much easier to have a discussion about a book than to explain all of the concepts to them over a series of conversations. Why do that level of work when the work is already done for you?

TWIN SOUL TELEPATHY

CAN I EXPERIENCE VISIONS AND DREAMS ABOUT MY TWIN SOUL?

This happens and yes, it'll make you feel crazy!

Please know that this is normal and is often your higher power attempting to share information with you. Additionally, these experiences come to you for a reason, often for behind-the-scenes healing that helps both of you and your connection.

Naturally, you'll want to share these visions with your twin soul or other people close to you. It can be helpful if you have a close friend or two with whom you have a spiritual connection to.

Depending on your connection and the relationship you have with your twin, it is your choice whether to tell them about these visions or not, but don't expect much of a response! Often, if one twin is not ready to receive information about the connection, that information will cascade right past them with very little notice or attention. Unless they are ready to experience these signs and synchronicities themselves, they will be like the hosts in the TV show *Westworld*. "Doesn't look like anything to me."

CAN I EXPERIENCE TELEPATHY WITH MY TWIN SOUL?

Absolutely. Your higher power is extremely efficient at getting messages between twin souls, so when they're blocked at moving the relationship forward in the physical, they will send messages between twin souls telepathically. These messages are usually around healing core wounds and breaking through the illusion of separation by sharing messages of love.

I recently had a telepathic message not from my twin soul, but from an ex. I had believed for a long time that we had broken up because I was too embarrassing to him—too loud, too opinionated, too experimental, too know-it-all, and too clumsy. I felt like I always did and said the wrong thing and he judged me for it. Shortly after this wounding was brought to my attention, I received a clear message from him in a dream state that no, he had always loved me in spite of the silly or embarrassing things I did. It hurt him that I believed he didn't or was that shallow.

This was not a typical dream—it was vivid and

visceral, and the message was clear. This is the type of content you can expect as you open yourself to telepathic and psychic experiences. It's very important that you don't question these messages when you receive them, because they are a test of your belief in your higher power and the Twin Soul Trinity.

OTHER COMMON MAJOR UPSETS ON THE JOURNEY

WHAT IS THE RUNNER-CHASER DYNAMIC?

The runner-chaser dynamic is an external illusion rooted in focusing too much on what's happening in the physical world. You and your true twin soul are one consciousness, so if they are running, you are also running. This may manifest in different ways in the physical reality, which gives an illusion of them running away and you chasing after them, or vice-versa. In truth, you are both running from yourselves, possibly in different areas of your life.

You can always heal this dynamic because it's just a distorted pattern in your consciousness. You each hold one portion of the distorted pattern that has you trapped in the dynamic. You can heal this using the tools in this book. If you'd like to go deeper into understanding this dynamic, I have done multiple videos about running and chasing at http://cardread-ingqueen.com/twin-flame-dynamic

WHAT IS A DARK NIGHT OF THE SOUL?

A dark night of the soul is a period that feels painful and depressing on this journey. When I have experienced it, it is usually a feeling of hopelessness and going into the darkest crevices of my mind. Others may experience it differently. You will know it's a dark night of the soul because it's existential and spiritually-related, rather than having anything to do with a bad day or an event in your life.

Typically, a dark night of the soul is tied to the Upheaval Phase from the 5U Healing Process. I've had my dark nights last anywhere from less than a day all the way to months on end. I find myself going into a dark night of the soul when I've healed some big stuff. Typically, I have to sit with it for a while and go deep with all of the massive shifts that are happening inside me.

To get through a dark night of the soul, I take these steps:

- **I make sure it's a dark night rather than depression -** I am someone who has suffered from bouts of depression all of my life and know how to manage true depression. If you are depressed, please don't assume it's a dark night of the soul and please seek professional treatment. A dark night of the soul is going to be clearly related to doing and moving through your soul work.

- **I allow myself to FULLY feel my emotions, no matter how dark they are -** For me, my emotions do get very dark, and if I hadn't seen the end of the tunnel on many dark nights of the soul, I would probably be concerned about even going there. In my last dark night of the soul, I found myself believing that I was completely worthless to my child. Emotionally, I wonder how I could ever provide for him what he needed around love, attention, discipline, caregiving, and support. There was zero evidence in the physical that I was worthless to him—quite the opposite as I am a hands on, gentle, loving, and supportive mom. I found myself able to hold the truth—that I am a great mom—and still feel the emotions—that I am a worthless mom. In truth, you are not your thoughts nor your emotions, so you can create a safe space to observe them at any time.

- **I allow the dark night of the soul to pass emotionally without taking action -** Feel all the emotions, then think about what your higher power is trying to tell you or show you. It does not make sense to examine your dark night of the soul while in the thick of it.

- **Once the dark night has passed emotionally, I allow myself to analyze what happened -** specifically, I like to look at what is the truth, what was I emotionally feeling was the truth, and how can I heal those emotions or upsets that were coming up? In the most recent case, feelings of worthlessness are common on my journey as it's a core wound—possibly *the* core wound—for me. So it's no surprise that it eventually came up for my child, whom I gave birth to in fall of 2019. Additionally, this dark night of the soul came on shortly after a huge energy clearing session, so I knew I was healing and releasing a lot around worthiness. In the physical, this manifested as thoughts and emotions about my worthiness to my child, but that piece really didn't matter—I was really just releasing more unworthiness in general.

- **I heal the upsets -** If there is anything lingering that I don't understand, I take the time to really write it out using the 5U Healing Process. This is so important as manifesting a dark night of the soul is a big communication from your higher power, trying to direct you to your next piece of healing.

- **I take action (if needed) -** Sometimes there are action items after a dark night of the soul. After my last one, I knew I had to start speaking up for myself about some things in several of my relationships, including with my twin soul, that I had been holding back. In some cases, I received love back, while in other cases, I didn't, but it didn't matter, as the point of it was to be honest, be heard, and communicate.

For more resources on this process of navigating the dark night of the soul, please take a look at my page of resources here: http://cardreadingqueen.com/dark-night-of-the-soul/

WHY DOES IT FEEL LIKE MY TWIN IS ATTRACTED TOWARD ME IN EVERY WAY, BUT STILL WON'T COMMIT IN THE PHYSICAL?

First, let me gently ask: do they feel attracted in every way if they won't commit in the physical? Unfortunately, there is no logical answer to this but no, they doesn't. That means that there is something in the union that is still repelling them.

Please don't take this to mean they are rejecting you, because that's not it at all. When I say "repelling," all I mean is that there's a place within the union where the two of you are not in alignment with the specific goal of uniting in the physical in a committed relationship.

That means that there is more healing to do. No

commitment in the 3D equals repellant desires and forces in the union. As I shared in the chapter on boundaries, the only way to shift into alignment is to acknowledge and heal all that is still repelling your twin from you.

WHAT IF IT ENDED BADLY BETWEEN MY TWIN SOUL AND ME?

If you believe that a bad ending in the past has ruined your chances with your twin soul, you likely have some wounding to resolve around the situation. It's important for you to heal everything that went badly in the relationship from your perspective. This can be done without any contact with your ex, thankfully!

Here's a checklist of what you should investigate:

- **Understand why you broke up from an unemotional level -** There's no question that you have a story you've been telling yourself about why you and your twin soul broke up. Likely, you've painted them as the source of the problem and yourself as the victim or the one who walked away rejected. Almost always, both twin souls feel like they were rejected in some way, regardless of who broke up with whom. So how can you rewrite this story so that no one is at fault and no one is rejected? This is the first step. It may take some effort, but it's important to come up with a story that meets these two criteria. Furthermore, you must believe in the possibility of this story, regardless of what your counterpart has told you. Remember, the 3D is an illusion!

- **Understand your part in the breakup -** Now, it's time to look at your part in the breakup. Where did you drive your twin soul away? What were you healing through this first iteration of your relationship? Where did they cause you pain, and what healing had you not yet done on yourself to allow that pain? Where did you run from them? For this step, you want to relate all your actions and reactions back to your own healing. Assume that if they hurt you, it was due to your own unhealed wounds. Assume that if you hurt them, it was due to your own unhealed wounds. What is the truth that you know in your heart about the breakup and your part in it?

- **Understand why you did what you did to the person and why they did what they did to you -** If you broke up with them, if you cheated on them, if you abandoned them, if you betrayed them, and more.... Or, if they did those things to you—what really happened? - Now, you want to look deeper at your own wounding and tie each specific wound to a broader core wound. For example, if you cheated on your twin soul, where did you experience betrayal in your own life? If your twin soul broke up with you, where did you experience abandonment in your own life?

- **Find empathy for why they did what they did to you and choose the kindest explanation -** We always choose the worst explanation when it comes to our twin soul and how they hurt us! For example, if your twin soul ghosted you, maybe you decide to believe that they don't love you anymore, when in reality they are in too much pain to stay in contact with you. The truth is, you don't know. Choose to believe the better story—it's really that simple! On this journey, it's important to believe in the best of your twin soul's motives and intentions. If you can't, identify areas where you don't and figure out why you don't. Heal the worst explanation that you've told yourself... because that story is the one inside you that you've chosen based on the information you have.

Only if you get to a good place with your twin soul (you feel completely at peace with your previous relationship and don't bring that forward to a new relationship), should you contact them to apologize or try to dissect your relationship together.

WHAT IF I BETRAYED MY TWIN SOUL AND THEY WON'T FORGIVE ME OR THEY SAY IT'S OVER FOREVER?

Twin souls will always forgive each other when they first forgive themselves!

- Why did you betray your twin soul? Use the Reflection Journaling Practice to heal all the reasons.

- Why won't they forgive you? Think of all the possibilities (and ask them, if possible) and systematically heal them using the Reflection Journaling Practice.

If you don't believe this will work to clear your energies, there may be some additional healing to do around faith, trust, boundaries, and the Twin Soul Trinity.

HOW DO I BUILD MY CONNECTION WITH MY TWIN SOUL WHEN WE LIVE APART?

When you feel called, reach out. When you don't, don't! There's actually no difference in building a connection long-distance. The long-distance is merely a symbol of a wounding pattern that the two of you have. It can be healed by asking yourself, what is this a symbol of in my relationship? How do I feel about the distance? How is it triggering me?

I had a long-distance relationship and I made it to mean that the person didn't love me and didn't truly want to commit to me long-term. Of course, those were just wounds within me that I was able to heal using the 5U Healing Process and the Reflection Journaling Practice.

So should you move or ask them to move? The answer really only lies within, in the question, where do you truly desire to live? Do you trust that as you step more deeply into yourself, you attract your twin soul to you?

WHY DOES THE TWIN SOUL DANCE FEEL HOT/COLD, PUSH/PULL, ONE STEP FORWARD, TWO STEPS BACK?

You may notice that the twin soul journey feels like a rollercoaster—up, down, side-to-side, topsy turvy, tumbling emotions. Here's what's going on:

- **Twin is hot/cold -** Your twin is happy and flirty with you in one instance, sometimes even pursuing a physical connection, then the next instance they've pulled back. This can happen across communication (friendly and connected, then ghosted), across affection (touchy-feely, then no contact), or across action (asks you out on date, then is silent for weeks). What's happening is that contact of any sort with your twin soul brings up wounding for clearing. Your twin is ecstatic to be with you, and at the same time needs to pull back after contact with you to clear and integrate the healing. This is especially true for physical romantic contact, as sex is just an ascension tool.

- **Twin is push/pull -** Your twin is sometimes in a tug-of-war with you about things like acknowledging your connection, defining your relationship, setting boundaries with each other, and even how much they contact you (or don't). Sometimes you are shoving your twin forward into the unknown, and sometimes you are dragging them kicking and screaming as you lead the way. What's happening is there is massive tension in the connection due to triggering. The universe and your souls do this to break through resistance and gently nudge the connection forward at the appropriate pace.

- **Twin is one step forward, two steps back -** You feel like you've made progress with your twin, but instead of charging forward after a victory, they pull back and seem to revert to the old, previous behavior. In truth this part of the dance is two steps forward, one step back, which makes all the difference. What's happening is your souls are trying to bal-

ance forward movement to protect the connection. You are trying to charge ahead too
quickly, while your twin is trying to baby step
forward too slowly. Both are ultimately the
two of you being in resistance to the journey.
This can also be your twin soul choosing to
heal through contrast, while you are healing
through inner work. It's the same thing...
your twin soul journey is slowed down in the
physical as the wounding needs to come up in
an appropriate divine order to be healed.

There is nothing to worry about in any of these
cases, as you cannot sever or mess up your connection to your twin. Have patience and surrender, as
these types of frustrations are always teaching you to
release control over the situation. Once you finally
do, the energy will move forward.

WHAT IF MY TWIN SOUL GETS ENGAGED? MARRIED? HAS A BABY?

First, I send my love and sympathy to you as I
know that these can be incredibly painful events and
major Tower Moments on your journey.

There is likely something about your twin soul
finding happiness and building his/her life with
someone else that is like a knife to the gut. You wonder, how did this happen? I've been doing my heal-

ing like a champ, and all it's done is driven my twin soul deeper into someone else's arms!

Although each of these instances (and many like them) can feel like a massive Game Over sign on your twin soul journey, nothing could be further from the truth.

In fact, if you've studied tarot, you'll know that The Tower (the strongest energy of Tower Moments on the twin soul journey) is not necessarily a negative card. It only means that you will encounter a life-changing surprise, which can include negative surprises like a car accident or a health scare, AND happy events, like a marriage proposal, a wedding, or a pregnancy.

All Tower Moments happen in your union to incite rapid trigger + healing and push you both forward into a new phase of your union.

ENGAGEMENT AND MARRIAGE

Engagement and marriage are social constructs that have very little to do with the spiritual realm. An engagement can be broken off in a conversation and in many states, you can end a marriage in less than a month with a bit of paperwork. It is never up to you to break up your twin soul's engagement or marriage. In fact, your twin soul's partner is in the picture for both your healing and theirs.

While you may not know specifically what your twin soul and their current partner are healing together, you can do your side of the healing work.

Release all jealousy, fear, resentment, anxiety, and comparison around this partner. You have manifested him or her into your twin soul's life to help you clear any attachment you have to being in a romantic relationship with your twin soul. To be clear, this doesn't mean you will not be in a romantic relationship with your twin soul, because you will! You are releasing the illusion of earthly constructs and believing in the spiritual truth of your union.

Additionally, release all possessiveness, attention-seeking, control, and obsessiveness around your twin soul. As you loosen your own energy around your twin soul and his/her partner, their bond will naturally release as well (as long as they are your true twin soul).

CHILDREN WITH ANOTHER

Children are other twin souls who come to Earth to experience the duality of this world. Each soul chooses other souls on earth to care for them, love them, and protect them while their bodies and ego minds are not of age to act independently. This does not indicate the age of the soul or your relationship to them in the 5D.

If your twin soul has a child, please know that the child has, at the 5D level, chosen both of you to be his or her guides in this lifetime. Please don't take this beyond what is it, of course, as this is not an invitation to make yourself a part of this child's physical life without their parents' permission! I only say this to make it clear that you and your twin soul have chosen this child and this child has chosen you. You have soul contracts in place and a child in the union is always a beautiful blessing and nothing to fear.

Earthly circumstances can change at any moment, so stay high vibe through these Tower Moments and see through the illusion. It is happening for your highest good.

JOURNALING PROMPTS

- What other questions do you have about your twin soul journey? Is there something you wish I had covered? Feel free to drop me a message at team@cardreadingqueen.com if you would like to submit your question as an episode topic for my Card Reading Queen Youtube channel and Your Twin Soul Journey podcast.

- What other support or resources do you wish were included in this book? How can you get the support you truly need to continue your journey, long after you've closed this book?

FEELING STUCK?

- **Check out the free Your Twin Soul Journey podcast**, where I produce 100+ episode seasons every year on a variety of twin flame and twin soul topics. If I haven't answered your question in this chapter, I may have answered it there. I also go into greater depth on many of these questions and continue to produce new content weekly. Listen on your commute to work, at your daily workout, or when you are doing chores around the house. You can learn more about the podcast here: http://cardreadingqueen.com/ytsj-podcast/

- **Subscribe to my free Card Reading Queen Youtube channel** where I post lots of tarot and astrology readings to help you understand the twin soul collective energies. You can find my channel here: http://cardreadingqueen.com/youtube

- **Find more books** about specific challenges you may be facing on the twin soul journey through my *Twin Soul Hearts in Union* book series. You can find the books we have on offer here: http://cardreadingqueen.com/books

Chapter Fourteen

NEXT STEPS ON YOUR TWIN SOUL JOURNEY

G oing deeper on your twin soul journey and with this work can sometimes feel a little scary, stressful, or overwhelming. You may also feel like it's not worth the effort or like you just want to be done with it all.

You may also be thinking, "I got what I needed from this resource, I can do the rest on my own!" I've seen for myself that is not the case; I've actually needed to give myself more support as I've continued to go along. The more I learn on this journey, the more I invest in my continued learning and understanding of it. Why would that be?

As you go deeper into something, you may have more questions and challenges that can't be solved through ordinary means like an internet search or a book. For me, I have typically figured out the basics on any given topic through reading several articles or watching several Youtube videos. Because I want to go deeper than basic, however, I sometimes find I need a more personalized solution that speaks to my specific situation. I can usually get this through an energy healing session or from my certified twin flame coaches.

Additionally, as you go deeper on this journey, you are expanding in your ability to give—to yourself, to your twin soul, to your higher power. You can't give without receiving because they are the same energy, so you need to expand in your ability to receive as well. As your ability to support your union expands, so must your ability to receive support for your union. This is very natural and a part of the ascension and healing process. Giving and receiving is an important masculine-feminine balancing that must happen in the union before uniting.

Lastly, I've found that every time I get more support, I also get hit with a ton of new blocks! This first happened to me when I did an Atlantean healing session with Kelly from Purple Priestess. It happened again when I signed up for coaching with twin flames José and Michaela. When you call in more support, it begs to be integrated... which means that it'll trigger your wounds again to help you heal to a deeper level so you can hold the support permanently.

WHAT ADDITIONAL SUPPORT DO YOU DESIRE?

You've already gotten support on this journey, which shows you desire help on this journey. Why not keep going? If this book has helped you, won't additional resources help you even more?

Every chapter of this book contains a list of resources to help you get unstuck. I encourage you to go back and review those chapters so you can see that support is available to you.

Additionally, I encourage you to support yourself around the material in this book by grabbing the complementary resources I've created, including the *Your Twin Soul Journey Workbook* and the *Your Twin Soul Journey Oracle Deck*. Both of these gorgeous companions to this book are available at http://card-readingqueen.com/twinsouljourney.

ADDITIONAL RESOURCES FOR TWIN SOUL AND SPIRITUAL WORK

A book cannot be complete without sharing its lineage of thought. There are many ideas that came together to form this book and it's important that you can trace the ideas I've presented to you here back to their original sources, which will themselves have original sources. Here are the people who have helped me deeply on this journey, that I wholeheartedly recommend:

- Susan Dawn at Susan Dawn Spiritual Connections, who is one of my oldest and dearest friends, soul sister, and a gifted twin flame message channeler and medium.

- José and Michaela Sanchez, who are certified twin flame ascension coaches and whom I am currently a client of at the time of writing this book.

- Kelly from the Purple Priestess, who specializes in an Atlantean Healing modality that has helped me make major shifts with just a single session.

- Jeff and Shaleia Divine from Twin Flames Universe, who wrote the book *Twin Flames: Finding Your Ultimate Lover*. I have recommended this book to many who find themselves on the twin flame journey.

I also highly recommend the books *Existential Kink* by Carolyn Elliot, *Light is the New Black* by Rebecca Campbell, and *Breaking the Habit of Being Yourself* by Joe Dispenza. These books were integral for me in understanding many aspects of the twin soul journey.

ADDITIONAL RESOURCES FOR DIVINE PURPOSE

I truly came to this work through the ascension process toward my divine purpose, which is where I first went all in with my higher power. Some of my greatest influences around my divine purpose include Steve Pavlina, Nisha Moodley, Tim Ferriss, Emerson Spartz, and Sean Platt and Johnny B. Truant. I have done extensive coaching with almost all of these mentors. You can find each of them and their bodies of work through a simple internet search.

THANK YOU

Thank you so much for reading this book to the end. I hope you have gained something for it that shifts your energy and helps you move forward on your ascension journey. Have a beautiful and blessed day and please check out the other books in the *Twin Soul Hearts in Union* series.

http://cardreadingqueen.com/books/

ACKNOWLEDGEMENTS

Thank you to the twin flame community at large, as I have learned so much from so many of you that made this book possible.

Thank you to my dedicated viewers, listeners, and readers, who make Card Reading Queen the most interesting and personal business I own.

Thank you to my dearest friend and soul sister Susan Dawn, who has truly been with me through thick and thin on this journey. (Since 2007!) It's no surprise that we continue to go through life together in synchronicity. I'm so grateful for our friendship and our soul family!

Thank you to my twin soul and my higher power—without you both, we couldn't have channeled this book together.

And finally, thank you to my beautiful family. I adore and love you all to the ends of the world.

ABOUT THE AUTHOR

Monica Grace has always been fascinated by card reading, the same way she's fascinated by stories. Card reading is a way to tell stories by taking each page of a book and laying it out in a new order every time.

She wrote her first story involving tarot cards in 2014, called *The Crown Reading*. She acquired her first oracle decks in 2016, the same year she began seriously studying tarot. She now reads cards for fun, pleasure, and insights from the Universe and God.

Tarot and oracle card reading was one of the gateways into Monica's spiritual awakening. She shares her readings, spreads, tips, and resources to help spread intuition, magic, and fun to the world.

Monica lives in a very, very old, 3-story home in St. Louis, MO with her husband and adorable westie, Mia. It possibly has ghosts. And definitely has a secret passage!

Visit CardReadingQueen.com for email updates and additional resources.

Made in the USA
Monee, IL
30 September 2020